HISTORY OF LEGENDARY WEAPONS

THIS BOOK WILL TELL YOU ABOUT THE RICH HISTORY OF LEGENDARY WEAPONS.

ARYAN SINGH

ISBN 979-888606017-1

I dedicate this book to Our Prime Minister Shri Narendra Modi Ji. He is the best man in this whole country. He understands what people exactly need. So I dedicate this book to him because he himself is more legendary than the weapons .

Contents

Foreword

This book will tell you about the rich history of legendary weapons.

Preface

The motive for writing this book is to revive old and legendary weapons. They are better than guns.

Acknowledgements

I would like to thank my mom , dad and brother for encouraging me to write this book.

Prologue

So get ready to know about the rich weapon history.

CHAPTER ONE

Karambit Knife

Double Karambits

The karambit or kerambit (as used in Indonesian), kurambik or karambiak (both from the Minangkabau language) is a small Indonesian curved knife resembling a claw from Minangkabau people of West Sumatra. Kerambit is one of the weapons commonly used in pencak silat.[1]

The karambit is believed to have originally been weaponized among the Minangkabau people of West Sumatra[2] where, according to folklore, it was inspired by the claws of a tiger. As with most weapons of the region, it was originally an agricultural implement designed to rake roots, gather threshing and plant rice in most of island Southeast Asia. It's a smaller variant of the Southeast Asian sickles (Filipino garab and karit; Indonesian celurit, arit, or sabit; and Malaysian sabit). As it was weaponised, the blade became more curved to maximise cutting potential. Through Indonesia's trade network and close contact with neighbouring countries, the weaponization of the karambit was eventually dispersed through what are now Thailand, Cambodia, Laos, Myanmar and the Philippines.[3][4]

Culturally, the karambit was a subject of condescension in Java because of its history as a weapon of the agrarian peasantry, as opposed to the kesatria (warrior class) who were trained in the keraton or royal palace. European accounts tell that soldiers in Indonesia were armed with a kris at their waist or back and a spear in their hands, while the karambit was used as a last resort when the fighter's other weapons were lost in battle. The renowned Bugis warriors of Sulawesi were famous for their embrace of the karambit. Today it is one of the main weapons of silat and is commonly used in Filipino martial arts as well.[5]

Superficially, the karambit resembles the jambiyah but there is no connection. The jambiyah was always designed as a weapon and serves as a status marker, often made by skilled artisans and jewelers using precious stones and metals, whereas the karambit was and still remains an unadorned, modest farmer's implement and useful utility knife.[5]

Technique

A modern karambit, held in a hammer grip (up) and the other held traditionally (down).

The karambit is held with the blade pointing downward from the bottom of the fist, usually curving forwards. While it is primarily used in a slashing or hooking motion, karambit with a finger ring are also used in a punching motion hitting the opponent with the finger ring. Some karambit are designed to be used in a hammering motion. This flexibility of striking methods is what makes it useful in self-defense situations. The finger guard makes it difficult to disarm and allows the knife to be maneuvered in the fingers without losing one's grip.[5]

The short Filipino karambit has found some favor in the West because such proponents allege the biomechanics of the weapon allow for more powerful cutting strokes and painful "ripping" wounds, and because its usability is hypothesized as more intuitive, but more difficult to master than a classic knife.

Variations

An 18th-19th century Malayan style Karambit (left), an 18th-19th century Sulawesi style Karambit (top) and a 16th-19th century Sumatran style Karambit (bottom).

There are many regional variants of karambit. The length of the blade, for example, could vary from one village or blacksmith to another. Some have no finger guard and some feature two blades, one on each side of the handle. Traditional types include:

Kuku Bima: Bhima's claw from West Java

Kuku Hanuman: Hanuman's claw from West Java

Kuku Macan: tiger's claw, endemic to Sumatra, Central Java and Madura

Kerambit Sumbawa: larger, sturdier kerambit made specially for battle. From the Sumba Islands

Kerambit Lombok: larger, sturdier kerambit made specially for battle. From Lombok

Lawi Ayam: chicken's claw, created by the Minang community

Additionally, modern karambit may have spikes or spurs on the front or rear ricasso, which may be intended for gripping clothing or horse tack, tearing flesh or for injecting a poison, such as the upas.[6]

Modern forms

The modern Western interpretation of the karambit is far removed from the original agricultural tool. They may have folding blades, are finished to a high standard, made from expensive materials as opposed to being rudimentary and makeshift and are generally larger to accommodate larger hands.[7]

CHAPTER TWO

Katana

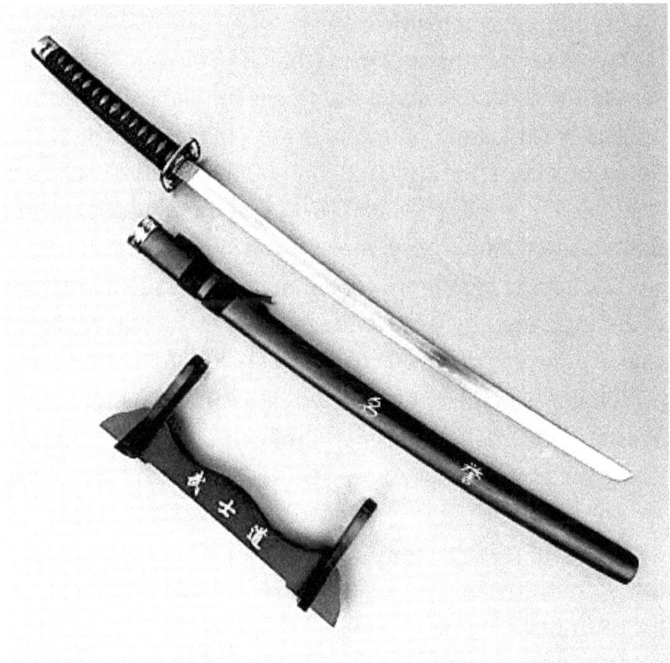

Katana

A katana (刀 or かたな or カタナ) is a Japanese sword characterized by a curved, single-edged blade with a circular or squared guard and long grip to accommodate two hands. Developed later than the tachi, it was used by samurai in feudal Japan and worn with the edge facing upward. Since the Muromachi period, many old tachi were cut from the root and shortened, and the blade at the root was crushed and converted into katana. The official term for katana in Japan is uchigatana (打刀) and the term katana (刀) often refers to single-edged swords from around the world.

Etymology and loanwords

Japanese Edo period wood block print (ca 1735) of a samurai with a tachi and a wakizashi (or kodachi).

The word katana first appears in Japanese in the Nihon Shoki of 720. The term is a compound of kata ("one side, one-sided") + na ("blade"),[6][7][8] in contrast to the double-sided tsurugi. See more at the Wiktionary entry.

The katana belongs to the nihontō family of swords, and is distinguished by a blade length (nagasa) of more than 2 shaku, approximately 60 cm (24 in).[9]

Katana can also be known as dai or daitō among Western sword enthusiasts, although daitō is a generic name for any Japanese long sword, literally meaning "big sword".[10]

As Japanese does not have separate plural and singular forms, both katanas and katana are considered acceptable forms in English.[11]

Pronounced [katana], the kun'yomi (Japanese reading) of the kanji 刀, originally meaning single edged blade (of any length) in Chinese, the word has been adopted as a loanword by the Portuguese.[12] In Portuguese the designation (spelled catana) means "large knife" or machete.[12]

Description

Mei (signature) and Nakago (tang) of an Edo period katana

The katana is generally defined as the standard sized, moderately curved (as opposed to the older tachi featuring more curvature) Japanese sword with a blade length greater than 60.6 cm (23.86 inches) (Japanese 2 Shaku).[13] It is characterized by its distinctive appearance: a curved, slender, single-edged blade with a circular or squared guard (tsuba) and long grip to accommodate two hands.[13]

With a few exceptions, katana and tachi can be distinguished from each other, if signed, by the location of the signature (mei) on the tang (nakago). In general, the mei should be carved into the side of the nakago which would face outward when the sword was worn. Since a tachi was worn with the cutting edge down, and the katana was worn with the cutting edge up, the mei would be in opposite locations on the tang.[14]

Western historians have said that katana were among the finest cutting weapons in world military history.[15][16] However, the main weapons on the battlefield in the Sengoku period in the 15th century were yumi (bow), yari (spear) and tanegashima (gun), and katana and tachi were used only for close combat. During this period, the tactics changed to a group battle by ashigaru (foot soldiers) mobilized in large numbers, so naginata (pole weapon) and tachi became obsolete as weapons on the battlefield and were replaced by yari and katana.[17][18][19] In the relatively peaceful Edo period, katana increased in importance as a weapon, and at the end of the Edo period, shishi (political activists) fought many battles using katana as their main weapon. Throughout history, katana and tachi were often used as gifts between daimyo (feudal lord) and samurai, or as offerings to the kami enshrined in Shinto shrines, and symbols of authority and spirituality of samurai.[18][20][19][17]

History

See also: Japanese sword § History

The production of swords in Japan is divided into specific time periods:[21]

Jōkotō (ancient swords, until around 900)

Kotō (old swords from around 900–1596)

Shintō (new swords 1596–1780)

Shinshintō (newer swords 1781–1876)

Gendaitō (modern or contemporary swords 1876–present)

Kotō (Old swords)[edit]

Masamune forges a katana with an assistant (ukiyo-e)

A Sōshū school katana modified from a tachi forged by Masamune. As it was owned by Ishida Mitsunari, it was commonly called Ishida Masamune. Important Cultural Property. Tokyo National Museum

A Sōshū school katana modified from a tachi, Kiriha Sadamune, forged by Sadamune, son of Masamune. 14th century, Kamakura period. Important Cultural Property. Tokyo National Museum

Muramasa (勢州桑名住村正) from the Tokyo National Museum

Katana originates from sasuga (刺刀), a kind of tantō (short sword or knife) used by lower-ranking samurai who fought on foot in the Kamakura period (1185–1333). Their main weapon was a long naginata and sasuga was a spare weapon. In the Nanboku-chō period (1336－1392) which corresponds to the early Muromachi period (1336 – 1573), long weapons such as ōdachi were popular, and along with this, sasuga lengthened and finally became katana.[22][23] Also, there is a theory that koshigatana (腰刀), a kind of tantō which was equipped by high ranking samurai together with tachi, developed to katana through the same historical background as sasuga, and it is possible that both developed to katana.[24] The oldest katana in existence today is called Hishizukuri uchigatana, which was forged in the Nanbokuchō period, and was dedicated to Kasuga Shrine later.[1]

The first use of katana as a word to describe a long sword that was different from a tachi, occurs as early as the Kamakura Period.[13] These references to "uchigatana" and "tsubagatana" seem to indicate a different style of sword, possibly a less costly sword for lower-ranking warriors. Starting around the year 1400, long swords signed with the katana-style mei were made. This was in response to samurai wearing their tachi in what is now called "katana style" (cutting edge up). Japanese swords are traditionally worn with the mei facing away from the wearer. When a tachi was worn in the style of a katana, with the cutting edge up, the tachi's signature would be facing the wrong way. The fact that swordsmiths started signing swords with a katana signature shows that some samurai of that time period had started wearing their swords in a different manner.[25][26]

Traditionally, yumi (bows) were the main weapon of war in Japan, and tachi and naginata were used only for close combat. The Ōnin War in the late 15th century in the Muromachi period expanded into a large-scale domestic war, in which employed farmers called ashigaru were mobilized in large numbers. They fought on foot using katana shorter than tachi. In the Sengoku period (period of warring states) in the late Muromachi period, the war became bigger and ashigaru fought in a close formation using yari (spears) lent to them. Furthermore, in the late 16th century, tanegashima (muskets) were introduced from Portugal, and Japanese swordsmiths mass-produced improved products, with ashigaru fighting with leased guns. On the battlefield in Japan, guns and spears became main weapons in addition to bows. Due to the changes in fighting styles in these wars, the tachi and naginata became obsolete among samurai, and the katana, which was easy to carry, became the mainstream. The dazzling looking tachi gradually became a symbol of the authority of high-ranking samurai.[22][20][19]

On the other hand, kenjutsu (swordsmanship) that makes use of the characteristics of katana was invented. The quicker draw of the sword was well suited to combat where victory depended heavily on short response times. (The practice and martial art for drawing the sword quickly and responding to a sudden attack was called Battōjutsu, which is still kept alive through the teaching of Iaido.) The katana further facilitated this by being worn thrust through a belt-like sash (obi) with the sharpened edge facing up. Ideally, samurai could draw the sword and strike the enemy in a single motion. Previously, the curved tachi had been worn with the edge of the blade facing down and suspended from a belt.[13][27]

From the 15th century, low-quality swords were mass-produced under the influence of the large-scale war. These swords, along with spears, were lent to recruited farmers called ashigaru and swords were exported. Such mass-produced swords are called kazuuchimono, and swordsmiths of the Bisen school and Mino school produced them by division of labor.[22][28] The export of katana and tachi reached its peak during this period, from the late 15th century to early 16th century when at least 200,000 swords were shipped to Ming Dynasty China in official trade in an attempt to soak up the production of Japanese weapons and make it harder for pirates in the area to arm. In the Ming Dynasty of China, Japanese swords and their tactics were studied to repel pirates, and wodao and miaodao were developed based on Japanese swords.[2][29][30]

From this period, the tang (nakago) of many old tachi were cut and shortened into katana. This kind of remake is called suriage (磨上げ).[4] For example, many of the tachi that Masamune forged during the Kamakura period were converted into katana, so his only existing works are katana and tantō.[31]

Daishō style handachi sword mounting. 16th – 17th century, Azuchi–Momoyama or Edo period.

From the late Muromachi period (Sengoku period) to the early Edo period, samurai were sometimes equipped with a katana blade pointing downwards like a tachi. This style of sword is called handachi, "half tachi". In handachi, both styles were often mixed, for example, fastening to the obi was katana style, but metalworking of the scabbard was tachi style.[32]

In the Muromachi period, especially the Sengoku period, people such as farmers, townspeople, and monks could have a sword. However, in 1588 Toyotomi Hideyoshi banned farmers from owning weapons and conducted a sword hunt to forcibly remove swords from anyone identifying as a farmer.[24]

The length of the katana blade varied considerably during the course of its history. In the late 14th and early 15th centuries, katana blades tended to have lengths between 70 and 73 centimetres (28 and 29 in). During the early 16th century, the average length dropped about 10 centimetres (3.9 in), approaching closer to 60 centimetres (24 in). By the late 16th century, the average length had increased again by about 13 centimetres (5.1 in), returning to approximately 73 centimetres (29 in).[27]

Shintō (New swords)

Antique Japanese daishō, the traditional pairing of two Japanese swords which were the symbol of the samurai, showing the traditional Japanese sword cases (koshirae) and the difference in size between the katana (bottom) and the smaller wakizashi (top).

Swords forged after 1596 in the Keichō period of the Azuchi–Momoyama period are classified as shintō (New swords). Japanese swords after shintō are different from kotō in forging method and steel (tamahagane). This is thought to be because Bizen school, which was the largest swordsmith group of Japanese swords, was destroyed by a great flood in 1590 and the mainstream shifted to Mino school, and because Toyotomi Hideyoshi virtually unified Japan, uniform steel began to be distributed throughout Japan. The kotō swords, especially the Bizen school swords made in the Kamakura period, had a midare-utsuri like a white mist between hamon and shinogi, but in the swords after shintō it has almost disappeared. In addition, the whole body of the blade became whitish and hard. Almost no one was able to reproduce midare-utsurii until Kunihira Kawachi reproduced it in 2014.[33][34]

Sword fittings. Tsuba (top left) and fuchigashira (top right) made by Ishiguro Masayoshi in the 18th or 19th century. Kogai (middle) and kozuka (bottom) made by Yanagawa Naomasa in the 18th century, Edo period. Tokyo Fuji Art Museum.

As the Sengoku period (period of warring states) ended and the Azuchi-Momoyama period to the Edo period started, katana-forging also developed into a highly intricate and well-respected art form. Lacquered saya (scabbards), ornate engraved fittings, silk handles and elegant tsuba (handguards) were popular among samurai in the Edo Period, and eventually (especially when Japan was in peace time), katana became more cosmetic and ceremonial items than practical weapons.[35] The Umetada school led by Umetada Myoju who was considered to be the founder of shinto led the improvement of the artistry of Japanese swords in this period. They were both swordsmiths and metalsmiths, and were famous for carving the blade, making metal accouterments such as tsuba (handguard), remodeling from tachi to katana (suriage), and inscriptions inlaid with gold.[36]

During this period, the Tokugawa shogunate required samurai to wear Katana and shorter swords in pairs. These short swords were wakizashi and tantō, and wakizashi were mainly selected. This set of two is called a daishō. Only samurai could wear the daishō: it represented their social power and personal honour.[13][27][37] Samurai could wear decorative sword mountings in their daily lives, but the Tokugawa shogunate regulated the formal sword that samurai wore when visiting a castle by regulating it as a daisho made of a black scabbard, a hilt wrapped with white ray skin and black string.[38] Japanese swords made in this period are classified as shintō.[39]

Shinshintō (New new swords)

Daishō (Katana and Wakizashi) forged by Minamoto no Kiyomaro. 1848, Late Edo period. (not to scale)

Daishō for formal attire with black scabbard, hilt winding thread and white ray skin hilt, which were regulated by the Tokugawa Shogunate. Daishō owned by Uesugi clan. Late Edo period.

In the late 18th century, swordsmith Suishinshi Masahide criticized that the present katana blades only emphasized decoration and had a problem with their toughness. He insisted that the bold and strong kotō blade from the Kamakura period to the Nanboku-chō period was the ideal Japanese sword, and started a movement to restore the production method and apply it to Katana. Katana made after this is classified as a shinshintō.[39] One of the most popular swordsmiths in Japan today is Minamoto Kiyomaro who was active in this shinshintō period. His popularity is due to his timeless exceptional skill, as he was nicknamed "Masamune in Yotsuya" after his disastrous life. His works were traded at high prices and exhibitions were held at museums all over Japan from 2013 to 2014.[40][41][42]

The idea that the blade of a sword in the Kamakura period is the best has been continued until now, and as of the 21st century, 80% of Japanese swords designated as National treasure in Japan were made in the Kamakura period, and 70% of them were tachi.[43][44]

The arrival of Matthew Perry in 1853 and the subsequent Convention of Kanagawa caused chaos in Japanese society. Conflicts began to occur frequently between the forces of sonnō jōi (尊王攘夷派), who wanted to overthrow the Tokugawa Shogunate and rule by the Emperor, and the forces of sabaku (佐幕派), who wanted the Tokugawa Shogunate to continue. These political activists, called the shishi (志士), fought using a practical katana, called the kinnōtō (勤皇刀) or the bakumatsutō (幕末刀). Their katana were often longer than 90 cm (35.43 in) in blade length, less curved, and had a big and sharp point, which was advantageous for stabbing in indoor battles.[39]

Gendaitō (Modern or contemporary swords)[edit]

Meiji – World War II

Although the number of forged swords decreased in the Meiji period, many artistically excellent mountings were made. A wakizashi forged by Soshu Akihiro. Nanboku-chō period. (top) Wakizashi mounting, Early Meiji period. (bottom)

During the Meiji period, the samurai class was gradually disbanded, and the special privileges granted to them were taken away, including the right to carry swords in public. The Haitōrei Edict in 1876 forbade the carrying of swords in public except for certain individuals, such as former samurai lords (daimyō), the military, and the police.[45] Skilled swordsmiths had trouble making a living during this period as Japan modernized its military, and many swordsmiths started making other items, such as farm equipment, tools, and cutlery. The craft of making swords was kept alive through the efforts of some individuals, notably Miyamoto Kanenori (宮本包則, 1830–1926) and Gassan Sadakazu (月山貞一, 1836–1918), who were appointed Imperial Household Artist. The businessman Mitsumura Toshimo (光村利藻, 1877－1955）tried to preserve their skills by ordering swords and sword mountings from the swordsmiths and craftsmen. He was especially enthusiastic about collecting sword mountings, and he collected about 3,000 precious sword mountings from the end of the Edo period to the Meiji period. About 1200 items from a part of his collection are now in the Nezu Museum.[46][47][48]

Military action by Japan in China and Russia during the Meiji period helped revive interest in swords, but it was not until the Shōwa period that swords were produced on a large scale again.[49] Japanese military swords produced between 1875 and 1945 are referred to as guntō (military swords).[50]

Type 95, World War II era guntō

During the pre-World War II military buildup, and throughout the war, all Japanese officers were required to wear a sword. Traditionally made swords were produced during this period, but in order to supply such large numbers of swords, blacksmiths with little or no knowledge of traditional Japanese sword manufacture were recruited. In addition, supplies of the Japanese steel (tamahagane) used for swordmaking were limited, so several other types of steel were also used. Quicker methods of forging were also used, such as the use of power hammers, and quenching the blade in oil, rather than hand forging and water. The non-traditionally made swords from this period are called shōwatō, after the regnal name of the Emperor Hirohito, and in 1937, the Japanese government started requiring the use of special stamps on the tang (nakago) to distinguish these swords from traditionally made swords. During this period of war, older antique swords were remounted for use in military mounts. Presently, in Japan, shōwatō are not considered to be "true" Japanese swords, and they can be confiscated. Outside Japan, however, they are collected as historical artifacts.[45][49][51]

Post-World War II

Japanese girl practicing iaidō with a modern training katana or iaitō. This sword was custom-made in Japan to suit the weight and size of the student. The blade is made of aluminum alloy and lacks a sharp edge for safety reasons.

Between 1945 and 1953, sword manufacture and sword-related martial arts were banned in Japan. Many swords were confiscated and destroyed, and swordsmiths were not able to make a living. Since 1953, Japanese swordsmiths have been allowed to work, but with severe restrictions: swordsmiths must be licensed and serve a five-year apprenticeship, and only licensed swordsmiths are allowed to produce Japanese swords (nihonto), only two longswords per month are allowed to be produced by each swordsmith, and all swords must be registered with the Japanese Government.[52]

Outside Japan, some of the modern katanas being produced by western swordsmiths use modern steel alloys, such as L6 and A2. These modern swords replicate the size and shape of the Japanese katana and are used by martial artists for iaidō and even for cutting practice (tameshigiri).

Mass-produced swords including iaitō and shinken in the shape of katana are available from many countries, though China dominates the market.[53] These types of swords are typically mass-produced and made with a wide variety of steels and methods.

According to the Parliamentary Association for the Preservation and Promotion of Japanese Swords, organized by Japanese Diet members, many katana distributed around the world as of the 21st century are fake Japanese swords made in China. The Sankei Shimbun analyzed that this is because the Japanese government allowed swordsmiths to make only 24 Japanese swords per person per year in order to maintain the quality of Japanese swords.[54][55]

Many swordsmiths after the Edo period have tried to reproduce the sword of the Kamakura period which is considered as the best sword in the history of Japanese swords, but they have failed. Then, in 2014, Kunihira Kawachi succeeded in reproducing it and won the Masamune Prize, the highest honor as a swordsmith. No one could win the Masamune Prize unless he made an extraordinary achievement, and in the section of tachi and katana, no one had won for 18 years before Kawauchi.[34]

Types

Katana are distinguished by their type of blade:

Shinogi-Zukuri is the most common blade shape for Japanese katana that provides both speed and cutting power. It features a distinct yokote: a line or bevel that separates the finish of the main blade and the finish of the tip. Shinogi-zukuri was originally produced after the Heian period.

Shobu-Zukuri is a variation of shinogi-zukuri without a yokote, the distinct angle between the long cutting edge and the point section. Instead, the edge curves smoothly and uninterrupted into the point.

Kissaki-Moroha-Zukuri is a katana blade shape with a distinctive curved and double-edged blade. One edge of the blade is shaped in normal katana fashion while the tip is symmetrical and both edges of the blade are sharp.

Forging and construction

Main article: Japanese swordsmithing

Named parts of a katana

Cross sections of Japanese sword blade lamination methods

Typical features of Japanese swords represented by katana and tachi are a three-dimensional cross-sectional shape of an elongated pentagonal to hexagonal blade called shinogi-zukuri, a style in which the blade and the tang (nakago) are integrated and fixed to the hilt (tsuka) with a pin called mekugi, and a gentle curve. When a shinogi-zukuri sword is viewed from the side, there is a ridge line of the thickest part of the blade called shinogi between the cutting-edge side and the back side. This shinogi contributes to lightening and toughening of the blade and high cutting ability.[56]

Katana are traditionally made from a specialized Japanese steel called tamahagane,[57] which is created from a traditional smelting process that results in several, layered steels with different carbon concentrations.[58] This process helps remove impurities and even out the carbon content of the steel. The age of the steel plays a role in the ability to remove impurities, with older steel having a higher oxygen concentration, being more easily stretched and rid of impurities during hammering, resulting in a stronger blade.[59] The smith begins by folding and welding pieces of the steel several times to work out most of the differences in the steel. The resulting block of steel is then drawn out to form a billet.

At this stage, it is only slightly curved or may have no curve at all. The katana's gentle curvature is attained by a process of differential hardening or differential quenching: the smith coats the blade with several layers of a wet clay slurry, which is a special concoction unique to each sword maker, but generally composed of clay, water and any or none of ash, grinding stone powder, or rust. This process is called tsuchioki. The edge of the blade is coated with a thinner layer than the sides and spine of the sword, heated, and then quenched in water (few sword makers use oil to quench the blade). The slurry causes only the blade's edge to be hardened and also causes the blade to curve due to the difference in densities of the micro-structures in the steel.[27] When steel with a carbon content of 0.7% is heated beyond 750 °C, it enters the austenite phase. When austenite is cooled very suddenly by quenching in water, the structure changes into martensite, which is a very hard form of steel. When austenite is allowed to cool slowly, its structure changes into a mixture of ferrite and pearlite which is softer than martensite.[60][61] This process also creates the distinct line down the sides of the blade called the hamon, which is made distinct by polishing. Each hamon and each smith's style of hamon is distinct.[27]

Example of a hamon

After the blade is forged, it is then sent to be polished. The polishing takes between one and three weeks. The polisher uses a series of successively finer grains of polishing stones in a process called glazing, until the blade has a mirror finish. However, the blunt edge of the katana is often given a matte finish to emphasize the hamon.[27]

Appreciation

Historically, katana have been regarded not only as weapons but also as works of art, especially for high-quality ones. For a long time, Japanese people have developed a unique appreciation method in which the blade is regarded as the core of their aesthetic evaluation rather than the sword mountings decorated with luxurious lacquer or metal works.[62][63]

It is said that the following three objects are the most noteworthy objects when appreciating a blade. The first is the overall shape referred to as sugata. Curvature, length, width, tip, and shape of tang of the sword are the objects for appreciation. The second is a fine pattern on the surface of the blade, which is referred to as hada or jigane. By repeatedly folding and forging the blade, fine patterns such as fingerprints, tree rings and bark are formed on its surface. The third is hamon. Hamon is a white pattern of the cutting edge produced by quenching and tempering. The object of appreciation is the shape of hammon and the crystal particles formed at the boundary of hammon. Depending on the size of the particles, they can be divided into two types, a nie and a nioi, which makes them look like stars or mist. In addition to these three objects, a swordsmith signature and a file pattern engraved on tang, and a carving inscribed on the blade, which is referred to as horimono, are also the objects of appreciation.[62][63]

A Japanese sword authentication paper (Origami) from 1702 that Hon'ami Kōchū certified a tantō made by Yukimitsu in the 14th century as authentic.

The Hon'ami clan, which was an authority of appraisal of Japanese swords, rated Japanese swords from these artistic points of view. In addition, experts of modern Japanese swords judge when and by which swordsmith school the sword was made from these artistic points of view.[62][63]

Generally, the blade and the sword mounting of Japanese swords are displayed separately in museums, and this tendency is remarkable in Japan. For example, the Nagoya Japanese Sword Museum "Nagoya Touken World", one of Japan's largest sword museums, posts separate videos of the blade and the sword mounting on its official website and YouTube.[64][65]

Rating of Japanese swords and swordsmiths

In Japan, Japanese swords are rated by authorities of each period, and some of the authority of the rating is still valid today.

In 1719, Tokugawa Yoshimune, the 8th shogun of the Tokugawa shogunate, ordered Hon'ami Kōchū, who was an authority of sword appraisal, to record swords possessed by daimyo all over Japan in books. In the completed "Kyōhō Meibutsu Chō" (享保名物帳) 249 precious swords were described, and additional 25 swords were described later. The list also includes 81 swords that had been destroyed in previous fires. The precious swords described in this book were called "Meibutsu" (名物) and the criteria for selection were artistic elements, origins and legends. The list of "Meibutsu" includes 59 swords made by Masamune, 34 by Awataguchi Yoshimitsu and 22 by Go Yoshihiro, and these three swordsmiths were considered special. Daimyo hid some swords for fear that they would be confiscated by the Tokugawa Shogunate, so even some precious swords were not listed in the book. For example, Daihannya Nagamitsu and Yamatorige, which are now designated as National Treasures, were not listed.[43]

Katana forged by Nagasone Kotetsu. The letters inlaid with gold on the tang (nakago) indicated that Yamano Kauemon (山野加右衛門), the official executioner of the Tokugawa shogunate and examiner of sword cutting performance, cut the four human torso overlapped.[66]

Yamada Asaemon V, who was the official sword cutting ability examiner and executioner of the Tokugawa shogunate, published a book "Kaiho Kenjaku" (懐宝剣尺) in 1797 in which he ranked the cutting ability of swords. The book lists 228 swordsmiths, whose forged swords are called

"Wazamono" (業物) and the highest "Saijo Ō Wazamono" (最上大業物) has 12 selected. In the reprinting in 1805, one swordsmith was added to the highest grade, and in the major revised edition in 1830 "Kokon Kajibiko" (古今鍛冶備考), two swordsmiths were added to the highest grade, and in the end, 15 swordsmiths were ranked as the highest grade. The katana forged by Nagasone Kotetsu, one of the top-rated swordsmith, became very popular at the time when the book was published, and many counterfeits were made. In these books, the three swordsmiths treated specially in "Kyōhō Meibutsu Chō" and Muramasa, who was famous at that time for forging swords with high cutting ability, were not mentioned. The reasons for this are considered to be that Yamada was afraid of challenging the authority of the shogun, that he could not use the precious sword possessed by the daimyo in the examination, and that he was considerate of the legend of Muramasa's curse.[43][67]

A katana forged by Magoroku Kanemoto. (Saijo Ō Wazamono) Late Muromachi period. (top) Katana mounting, Early Edo period. (bottom)

At present, by the Law for the Protection of Cultural Properties, important swords of high historical value are designated as Important Cultural Properties (Jūyō Bunkazai, 重要文化財), and special swords among them are designated as National Treasures (Kokuhō, 国宝). The swords designated as cultural properties based on the law of 1930, which was already abolished, have the rank next to Important Cultural Properties as Important Art Object (Jūyō Bijutsuhin, 重要美術品). In addition, The Society for Preservation of Japanese Art Swords, a public interest incorporated foundation, rates high-value swords in four grades, and the highest grade Special Important Sword (Tokubetsu Juyo Token, 特別重要刀剣) is considered to be equivalent to the value of Important Art Object. Although swords owned by the Japanese Imperial Family are not designated as National Treasures or Important Cultural Properties because they are outside the jurisdiction of the Law for the Protection of Cultural Properties, there are many swords of the National Treasure class, and they are called "Gyobutsu" (御物).[43][68]

Currently, there are several authoritative rating systems for swordsmiths. According to the rating approved by the Japanese government, from 1890 to 1947, two swordsmiths who were appointed as Imperial Household Artist and after 1955, six swordsmiths who were designated as Living National Treasure are regarded as the best swordsmiths. According to the rating approved by The Society for Preservation of Japanese Art Swords, a public interest incorporated foundation, 39 swordsmiths who were designated as Mukansa (無鑑査) since 1958 are considered to be the highest ranking swordsmiths. The best sword forged by Japanese swordsmiths is awarded the most honorable Masamune prize by The Society for Preservation of Japanese Art Swords. Since 1961, eight swordsmiths have received the Masamune Prize, and among them, three swordsmiths, Masamine Sumitani, Akitsugu Amata and Toshihira Osumi, have received the prize three times each and Sadakazu Gassan II has received the prize two times. These four people were designated both Living National Treasures and Mukansa.[69]

Usage in martial arts

Katana were used by samurai both in the battlefield and for practicing several martial arts, and modern martial artists still use a variety of katana. Martial arts in which training with katana is used include iaijutsu, battōjutsu, iaidō, kenjutsu, kendō, ninjutsu and Tenshin Shōden Katori Shintō-ryū.[70][71][72] However, for safety reasons, katana used for martial arts are usually blunt edged, to reduce the risk of injury. Sharp katana are only really used during tameshigiri (blade testing), where a practitioner practices cutting a bamboo or tatami straw post.

Storage and maintenance

If mishandled in its storage or maintenance,

the katana may become irreparably damaged. The blade should be stored horizontally in its sheath, curve down and edge facing upward to maintain the edge. It is extremely important that the blade remain well-oiled, powdered and polished, as the natural moisture residue from the hands of the user will rapidly cause the blade to rust if not cleaned off. The traditional oil used is chōji oil (99% mineral oil and 1% clove oil for fragrance). Similarly, when stored for longer periods, it is important that the katana be inspected frequently and aired out if necessary in order to prevent rust or mold from forming (mold may feed off the salts in the oil used to polish the blade).[73]

World records

Multiple sword world records were made with a katana and verified by Guinness World Records. Iaido master Isao Machii set the record for "Most martial arts katana cuts to one mat (suegiri)",[74] "Fastest 1,000 martial arts sword cuts",[75] "Most sword cuts to straw mats in three minutes",[76] and "Fastest tennis ball (708km/h) cut by sword".[77] There are various records for Tameshigiri. For example the Greek Agisilaos Vesexidis set the record for most martial arts sword cuts in one minute (73) on 25 June

2016.[78]

Ownership and trade restrictions

Republic of Ireland

Under the Firearms and Offensive Weapons Act 1990 (Offensive Weapons) (Amendment) Order 2009, katanas made post-1953 are illegal unless made by hand according to traditional methods.[79]

United Kingdom

As of April 2008, the British government added swords with a curved blade of 50 cm (20 in) or over in length ("the length of the blade shall be the straight line distance from the top of the handle to the tip of the blade") to the Offensive Weapons Order.[80] This ban was a response to reports that samurai swords were used in more than 80 attacks and four killings over the preceding four years.[81] Those who violate the ban would be jailed up to six months and charged a fine of £5,000. Martial arts practitioners, historical re-enactors and others may still own such swords. The sword can also be legal provided it was made in Japan before 1954, or was made using traditional sword making methods. It is also legal to buy if it can be classed as a "martial artist's weapon". This ban applies to England, Wales, Scotland and Northern Ireland. This ban was amended in August 2008 to allow sale and ownership without licence of "traditional" hand-forged katana.[82]

CHAPTER THREE

Throwing Axes

Throwing Axe

A throwing axe is a weapon used from Antiquity to the Middle Ages by foot soldiers and occasionally by mounted soldiers. Usually, they are thrown in an overhand motion (much like throwing a baseball) in a manner that causes the axe to rotate as it travels through the air.Axe throwing is a sport in which the competitor throws an axe at a target, attempting to hit the bullseye as near as possible like that of the archery. Axe throwing is an event held in most lumberjack competitions. A skilled axe thrower will rotate the throwing axe exactly once throughout the flight so that the sharpened edge of the head will penetrate the target. Throwing axes are becoming popular among outdoor enthusiasts as a throwing tool.

Throwing axes have been used since prehistoric times and were developed into the francisca by the Franks in the 3rd century AD. Although generally associated with the Franks, it was also used by other Germanic peoples of the period including the Anglo-Saxons. The francisca is characterised by its distinctly arch-shaped head, widening toward the cutting edge and terminating in a prominent point at both the upper and lower corners. The top of the head is usually either S-shaped or convex with the lower portion curving inward and forming an elbow with the short wooden haft. Sometimes the head is more up-swept, forming a wider angle with the haft. Most franciscas have a round or teardrop-shaped eye designed to fit the tapered haft, similar to Viking axes. Even this New World weapon experienced some influence by the francisca in the French territories. Tomahawk throwing competitions still take place today.

Hurlbat

Main article: Hurlbat

A hurlbat (or whirlbat, whorlbat) is the term used for a type of weapon with unclear original definition. Older reference works refer to it largely as a type of club, either held in the hand or possibly thrown. Modern usage appears to refer to a type of throwing-axe.

Nzappa zap

Ceremonial axe, Songe people, Honolulu Museum of Art, 3023

Main article: Nzappa zap

The Nzappa zap is a weapon from the Democratic Republic of the Congo. This weapon is certainly one of the more unusual-looking throwing axes. The Nzappa zaps sometimes had an iron head with two or three human faces. The handle had the shape of a club with a round upper part. The head is attached to the club via struts, giving the weapon its unique design. Besides being thrown, these axes were sometimes used to injure the enemy directly by hand. This can be used both for short distances throw and as a melee weapon in hand-to-hand combat.

CHAPTER FOUR

Brass Knuckles

Brass Knuckle

Brass knuckles (variously referred to as knuckles, knucks, brass knucks, knucklebusters, knuckledusters, knuckle daggers, English punch, iron fist, paperweight, or a classic) are "fist-load weapons" used in hand-to-hand combat. Brass knuckles are pieces of metal shaped to fit around the knuckles. Despite their name, they are often made from other metals, plastics or carbon fibers. Designed to preserve and concentrate a punch's force by directing it toward a harder and smaller contact area, they result in increased tissue disruption, including an increased likelihood of fracturing the intended target bones on impact. The extended and rounded palm grip also spreads across the attacker's palm the counter-force that would otherwise be absorbed primarily by the attacker's fingers, reducing the likelihood of damage to the attacker's fingers. It also allows its user to break glass windows without injuring their hands, thus are widely utilized in vehicle theft to break car windows.

History and variations

Brass knuckles carried by Abraham Lincoln's bodyguards during his train ride through Baltimore. Ford's Theatre National Historic Site, 2007

An Apache revolver, a weapon that combines brass knuckles with a firearm and a dagger – Curtius Museum, Liège, 2011

Mark I brass knuckles Trench Knife

Homemade brass knuckles used in a lumber camp in Pine County, Minnesota. c. 1890

Metal ring and knuckle style weapons date back to ancient times and have been used all over the world for many hundreds of years. Vajra mushti has been practiced in India since at least the 12th century and mentioned in Manasollasa. The Nihang Sikhs used an early variant called

Sher Panja in the 18th century. Cast iron, brass, lead, and wood knuckles were made in the United States during the American Civil War (1861–1865). Soldiers would often buy cast iron or brass knuckles. If they could not buy them, they would carve their own from wood, or cast them at camp by melting lead bullets and using a mold in the dirt.

Some brass knuckles have rounded rings, which increase the impact of blows from moderate to severe damage. Other instruments (not generally considered to be "brass knuckles" or "metal knuckles" per se) may have spikes, sharp points and cutting edges. These devices come in many variations and are called by a variety of names, including "knuckle knives."

By the late 19th century, knuckledusters were incorporated into various kinds of pistols such as the Apache revolver used by criminals in France in the late 19th to early 20th centuries.[1] During World War I the US Army issued two different knuckle knives, the US model 1917 and US model 1918 Mark I trench knives. Knuckles and knuckle knives were also being made in England at the time and purchased privately by British soldiers. By World War II, knuckles and knuckle knives were quite popular with both American and British soldiers. The Model 1918 trench knives were reissued to American paratroopers. British Commandos even had their very own "Death's Head" knuckle knife, featuring a skull-shaped brass knuckle handle.

A notable knuckle knife still in use is the Cuchillo de Paracaidista, issued to Argentinian paratroopers. Current-issue models have an emergency blade in the crossguard.

Legality and distributionq

Brass knuckles are illegal in Hong Kong, Austria, Belgium, Canada, Denmark, Bosnia, Croatia,[2] Cyprus,

Finland, Germany,[3] Greece, Hungary, Israel, the Republic of Ireland,[4] Malaysia,[5][6] the Netherlands, Norway, Poland, Portugal, Russia, Spain,[7] Turkey,[8] Sweden, Singapore,[9] Republic of China in Taiwan,[10] and the United Kingdom.[11]

Import of brass knuckles into Australia is illegal unless a government permit is obtained; permits are available for only limited purposes, such as police and government use, or use in film productions.[12] They are prohibited weapons in the state of New South Wales.[13]

In Brazil, brass knuckles are legal and freely sold. They are called "soco inglês", which means "English punch".

In Canada, brass knuckles, or any similar devices made of metal, are listed as prohibited weapons;[14] possession of such weapon is a criminal offence under the Criminal Code.[15] Plastic knuckles have been determined to be legal in Canada.[16] Similar legislation has been instituted in Russia and Australia[citation needed].

In France, brass knuckles have been illegal for twenty years. They can be bought as a "collectable" (provided one is over 18), but it is forbidden to carry or use one, whatever the circumstance, self-defense included.[17] The French term is "poing américain", which literally means "American fist".[18]

In Germany, brass knuckles are by law "illegal weapons" ("Verbotene Waffen") and are forbidden for carry or possession in any known variant. The German term is "Schlagring", which literally means "punch ring".

In Italy and Mexico, brass knuckles are legal and freely sold to people of legal age (over 18 years old), but carrying them is forbidden.

In Russia, brass knuckles were illegal to purchase or own during times of Russian Empire and are still forbidden according to Article 6 of 1996 Federal Law On Weapons.[19] They are called "кастет" (French casse-tête, literally "head breaker").

In Sweden, brass knuckles are legal to purchase and own (for people 21 years of age) but are not legal to sell in stores or carry in public. The carrying of brass knuckles carries the same penalty as carrying a knife and falls under the same law. They are called "knogjärn", literally "knuckle iron".

In Serbia,[20] brass knuckles are legal to purchase and own (for people over 16 years old) but are not legal to carry in public. They are called "боксер" literally "boxer".

In the Republic of China in Taiwan, according to the Law of the Republic of China, possession and sales of brass knuckles are illegal. Under the regulation, brass knuckles are considered weapons. Without the permission of the central regulatory agency, it is against the law to manufacture, sell, transport, transfer, rent, or have them in a collection or on display.[10]

In the United States, brass knuckles are not significantly regulated at the federal level, but various state, county and city laws prohibit their purchase and/or possession. Some state laws require purchasers to be 18 or older. Most states have statutes regulating the carrying of weapons, and many specifically prohibit brass knuckles or "metal knuckles." Where they are legal, brass knuckles can normally be purchased online or at flea markets, swap meets, gun shows, and at some sword and weapon shops. Some companies manufacture belt buckles or novelty paper weights that function as brass knuckles and are sold "for entertainment purposes only".[21] Brass knuckles made of hardened plastic, rather than metal, have been marketed as "undetectable by airport metal detectors."[22] Several states that ban brass knuckles also ban plastic knuckles. New York's criminal law statutes list both "metal knuckles" and "plastic knuckles" as prohibited weapons but do not define either.[23]

Illegality of brass knuckles used to target minorities

Some laws in the United States making brass knuckles illegal have been used in such a manner as to target minorities that might otherwise have encountered police, but the mere possession of brass knuckles then serves as pretense for an arrest. Some states, such as the state of Texas,[24] have passed laws repealing earlier prohibitions on the ownership and carry of brass knuckles (and knuckles made from other materials used for defensive purposes). The use of brass knuckles as a weapon to initiate an attack is still criminalized, so only defensive use of brass knuckles is legalized. The carry of brass knuckles before the Texas law came into effect on September 1, 2019, resulted in the arrest of "93 people" in 2017, "...often used to target young people of color" said the sponsor of the bill, Democrat Joe Moody of El Paso to a Dallas Morning News correspondent.[24]

Prior to brass knuckles becoming regularly legal for carry, ownership, and possession in 2019, they were considered as regulated, or illegal, as "explosives" and "machine guns" according to a report by ABC News.[25]

CHAPTER FIVE

Kusarigama

Kusarigama

A kusarigama (Japanese: 鎖鎌, lit. "chain-sickle") is a traditional Japanese weapon that consists of a kama (the

Japanese equivalent of a sickle or billhook) on a kusari-fundo – a type of metal chain (kusari) with a heavy iron weight (fundo) at the end. The kusarigama is said to have been developed during the Muromachi period. The art of handling the kusarigama is called kusarigamajutsu.

History

The researcher Nawa Yumio believes that the kusarigama was based on the jingama, a tool that resembles a sickle which was used to cut through a horse's ropes in the case of a fire. The jingama could also be used as a weapon and according to Nawa, the tool might have been combined with a konpi (棍飛) which is a chain that contained a weighted end and a chain around the user's wrist. People would wield the weapons with both hands to protect their horses against criminals. Another theory is that the kusarigama is based on the tobiguchi (ja:鳶口), which is a type of axe that had a "stout haft and a short pick-like blade".[1]

There is no evidence of the kusarigama being used as a battlefield weapon in mass combat. Swinging its long chain could endanger allies and it would be ineffective against armor. The weapon is at its most useful when wielded against an opponent who attacks with a sword; it is not as useful against a longer weapon such as a spear, a naginata, or a bō.[1] Perhaps it was carried as a backup weapon, for its light weight. It is likely that the kusarigama was common during the Edo period, used against swordsmen and as a training weapon, but it was first created during the Muromachi period.[1][2]

From the 12th century until the time of the Tokugawa shogunate, many fighters specialized in the use of the weapon. One of these fighters was Yamada Shinryukan, a man who defeated many swordsmen; he was trapped in a bamboo grove by Araki Mataemon and killed. Yamada did not have enough room in the bamboo grove to swing around the chain of his kusarigama.[3] The weapon has been used by ninjas.[4] The kusarigama has also been used as a "plaything for warriors with time on their hands, and a means of attracting rural students who wished to do something unique in their local festivals".[1] Samurai women used the weapon as well.[5]

The schools of kenjutsu, jūjutsu, and naginatajutsu taught kusarigamajutsu, the art of handling the kusarigama. It combined the aspects of kamajutsu, kusarijutsu, and fundojutsu. Kamajutsu refers to the kama (sickle), kusarijutsu refers to the chain, and fundojutsu refers to the weight.[6] Kusari-fundo refers to the chain combined with the iron weight.[7][1]

A handle of a kusarigama is surrounded by raden which is a lacquer wood inlay that contains pieces of mother-of-pearl. The handle often has metal bands or strips for reinforcement at either end.[8]

Ellis Amdur's book Old School: Essays on Japanese Martial Traditions retells a myth about the origin of the kusarigama. In the story, a farmer who used a farming sickle to cut his rice plants was attacked by a samurai. The farmer used the sickle with a chain attachment to defeat the warrior. According to Amdur, trapping an opponent with the chain is not effective, and a farmer's sickle would be an awkward weapon. He also states that there is no evidence for peasant use of the kusarigama or that it was derived from a farmer's tool.[1] However, Donn F. Draeger mentions in his book Comprehensive Asian Fighting Arts that the sickle, referring to the kama, was originally used for agriculture and later became used as a weapon.[9]

Methods of use

Attacking with the weapon usually entailed swinging the weighted chain in a large circle over one's head, and then whipping it forward to entangle an opponent's spear, sword, or other weapon, or immobilizing their arms or legs. This allows the kusarigama user to easily rush forward and strike with the sickle.[10]

There are three types of kusarigama. The first type has a weapon in the shape of a sickle that has a chain attached to the end of its shaft. The use of the first type depends on the ryū (school), with the weapon being held in either hand and its chain and weight being held in the other hand to be swung at the other person. Depending on how easy it is to see the weapon's weight move, "it can be deflected or blocked". One hit with the kusarigama is typically not able to stop someone from attacking and the weight needs to be "reeled in" by the wielder again so that a second attack can be made. The second type of kusarigama has the chain "attached at the base of the blade" and it is much more powerful than the first type. The second type allows the wielder to use quick attacks and it can continue to be used if the weapon is deflected. It only takes one hand to operate the second type and the other hand can be used for another form of combat. The third type "has a straight blade, hafted at right angles, with a handguard set at the blade side". The chain is attached to the weapon's base and it is controlled with both hands, similar to the first type of kusarigama.[1]

Modern use

Issue 9 of This Is Japan by The Asahi Shimbun stated, "Perhaps the most unusual Japanese martial art is that which employs the kusarigama. The fact that it has survived through history gives mute testimony to its effectiveness. Yet, the casual observer, untrained in its use, would be apt to regard it as a foolish toy."[11] A book by Tadashi Yamashita that teaches people how to use the Okinawan kusarigama was advertised in the magazine Black Belt in the 1980s.[12][13]

In the Republic of Ireland, the kusarigama is classified as an illegal offensive weapon. The Firearms and Offensive Weapons Act 1990 in Ireland does not allow the kusarigama, and other similar weapons, to be manufactured, imported, or sold. These actions can result in becoming imprisoned for up to seven years.[14]

CHAPTER SIX

Shurinken

Shuriken

A shuriken (Japanese: 手裏剣; literally: "hidden hand blade") is a Japanese concealed weapon that was used as a hidden dagger or metsubushi to distract or misdirect.[1][2]

They are also known as throwing stars, or ninja stars, although they were originally designed in many different shapes. The major varieties of shuriken are the bō shuriken (棒手裏剣, stick shuriken) and the hira shuriken (平手裏剣, flat shuriken) or shaken (車剣, wheel shuriken, also read as kurumaken).

Shuriken were supplementary weapons to the sword or various other weapons in a samurai's arsenal, although they often had an important tactical effect in battle.[3][4][5][better source needed] The art of wielding the shuriken is known as shurikenjutsu[5] and was taught as a minor part of the martial arts curriculum of many famous schools, such as Yagyū Shinkage-ryū, Tenshin Shōden Katori Shintō-ryū, Ittō-ryū, Kukishin-ryū, and Togakure-ryū.[2][6][7]

Bo-shuriken

A Bo-shuriken is a throwing weapon consisting of a straight iron or steel spike, usually four-sided but sometimes round or octagonal in section. Some examples have points on both ends. The length ranges from 12 to 21 cm (5–8½ in) and the average weight from 35 to 150 grams (1.2–5.4 ounces).[8] They should not be confused with the kunai, which is a thrusting and stabbing implement that is sometimes thrown.

Bo-shuriken were constructed from a wide variety of everyday items, and as such came in many shapes and sizes. Some derived their names from the materials of which they were made, such as kugi-gata (nail form), hari-gata (needle form) and tantō-gata (knife form); some were named after an object of similar appearance, such as hoko-gata (spear form), matsuba-gata (pine-needle form); while others have names that are purely descriptive, such as kankyuto (piercing tool form), kunai-gata (utility tool form), or teppan (plate metal) and biao (pin).[8]

The bo-shuriken is thrown in a number of ways, such as overhead, underarm, sideways and rearwards, but in each case the throw involves the blade sliding out of the hand through the fingers in a smooth, controlled flight. The major throwing methods are the jiki da-ho (direct-hit method), and the han-ten da-ho (turning-hit method). These two are technically different, in that the former does not allow the blade to spin before it hits the target, while the latter requires that the blade spin.

Four antique forged Japanese bo shuriken (iron throwing darts with linen flights)

Other items such as hairpins, kogata (utility knife), and chopsticks were thrown in the same way as bo-shuriken, although they were not associated with any particular school of shurikenjutsu.

The origins of the bo-shuriken in Japan are still unclear despite continuing research. This is partly because shurikenjutsu was a secret art and also due to the fact that throughout early Japanese history there were many independent exponents of the skill of throwing long, thin objects. The earliest-known reference to a school teaching shurikenjutsu is to Ganritsu Ryu, active during the 17th century. This school utilized a long, thin implement with a bulbous head, thought to be derived from the arrow. Surviving examples of blades used by this school appear to combine an arrow's shape with that of a needle traditionally used in Japanese leatherwork and armor manufacture.[8]

There are earlier mentions in written records[clarification needed]—such as the Osaka Gunki (大阪軍記, the military records of Osaka)—of the standard knife and short sword being thrown in battle. Miyamoto Musashi is said to have won a duel by throwing his short sword at his opponent, killing him.

Hira shuriken/shaken

Various types of shuriken at the Iga-ryū Ninja Museum

Hira-shuriken generally resemble the popular conception of shuriken. They are constructed from thin, flat plates of metal derived from a variety of sources including hishi-gane (coins), kugi-nuki (carpentry tools), spools, and senban (nail removers).

They often have a hole in the center and possess a fairly thin blade sharpened mainly at the tip. The holes derive from their source in items that had holes—old coins, washers, and nail-removing tools. This proved convenient for the shuriken user as the weapons could be strung on a string or dowel in the belt for transport, and the hole also had aerodynamic and weighting effects that aided the flight of the blade.[8]

There are a wide variety of forms of hira-shuriken, and they are now usually identified by the number of points the blades possess. As with bo-shuriken, the various shapes of hira-shuriken were usually representative of a particular school (ryū) or region that preferred the use of such shapes, and it is therefore possible to identify the school by the type of blade used.[8]

Usage

Shuriken targets were primarily the more exposed parts of the body: the eyes, face, hands, or feet. The shuriken would sometimes be thrown in a way that slashed the opponent in a glancing blow and travelled on, becoming lost, leaving him confused about the cause of the wound.[3][7][better source needed] Shuriken, despite low mass, were capable of dealing lethal blows at short ranges. In some cases, shuriken were capable of partially disemboweling targets.[9]

Shuriken, especially hira-shuriken, were also used in novel ways—they could be embedded in the ground, injuring those who stepped on them (similar to a caltrop), wrapped in fuse to be lit and thrown to cause fire, or wrapped in a cloth soaked in poison and lit to cover an area with a cloud of poisonous smoke.[10] They could also be used as a handheld weapon in close combat.[11][better source needed]

There are reports of shuriken being coated with poison, intended either as a throwing weapon or to be left in a conspicuous place for a victim to pick up.[12][7][better source needed] Other reports indicate that shuriken may have been buried in dirt or animal feces and allowed to harbor the bacterium Clostridium tetani—if the point penetrated a victim deeply enough, the bacteria transferred into the wound could cause a then-incurable tetanus infection.[7]

Shuriken are simple weapons, but their historical value has increased.[6][7] Unlike the treasured katana and other bladed weapons, antique shuriken are not often well preserved, largely due to their expendable nature.[13]

Today

Modern shuriken are most often made of stainless steel and are commercially available in many knife shops in Europe and North America, or via the Internet. They are illegal to possess or carry in some countries, such as Belgium, the Netherlands, Canada,[14]

Germany,[15][better source needed] and the United Kingdom (manufacture, sale, distribution and import).[16] In the United States, some states prohibit them (e.g., California,[17] Indiana,[18] New York[19]) while others allow them. In some cases they may be allowed but are still subject to specific local legislation. Owners may be required to possess a certificate for the possession of knives.

CHAPTER SEVEN

Nunchaku

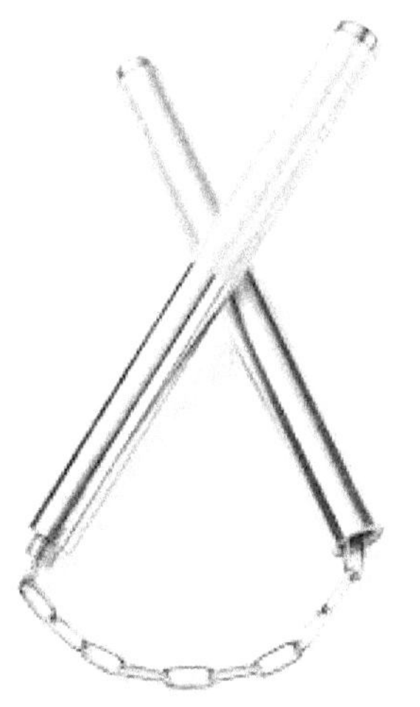

Nunchaku

he nunchaku (/nʌnˈtʃækuː/) (Japanese: ヌンチャク, sometimes "Dual Section Stick", "nunchuks"[1] (/ˈnʌntʃʌks/), "nunchucks",[2] "chainsticks",[3] "chuka sticks"[4] or "karate sticks"[5] in English,) is a traditional Okinawan martial arts weapon consisting of two sticks (traditionally made of wood), connected to each other at their ends by a short metal chain or a rope. A person who has practiced using this weapon is referred to in Japanese as nunchakuka.

The nunchaku is most widely used in martial arts such as Okinawan kobudō and karate. It is intended to be used as a training weapon, since practicing with it enables the development of quick hand movements and improves posture. Modern nunchaku may be made of metal, plastic or fiberglass instead of the traditional wood. Toy versions and replicas not intended to be used as weapons may be made of polystyrene foam or plastic. Possession of this weapon is illegal in some countries, except for use in professional martial arts schools.

The origin of the nunchaku is unclear; a traditional explanation holds that it was originally used by Okinawan farmers as a flail for threshing rice. Another weapon, called the tabak-toyok, native to the northern Philippines, is constructed very similarly, suggesting that it and the nunchaku descended from the same instrument. Even in the old days, when the nunchaku was used as a weapon, it was never widely popular, because it was ineffective against more widely used weapons of the time, such as katana and naginata - and little information about techniques for its use as a weapon survive.

In modern times, the nunchaku (Tabak-Toyok) was popularized by the actor and martial artist Bruce Lee and by Dan Inosanto.[6] Lee famously used nunchaku in several scenes in the 1972 film Fist of Fury.[7] When Tadashi Yamashita worked with Bruce Lee on the 1973 film Enter the Dragon, he enabled Lee to further explore the use of the nunchaku and other kobudo disciplines. The nunchaku is also the signature weapon of the cartoon character Michelangelo in the Teenage Mutant Ninja Turtles franchise.

In addition the nunchaku is used in certain contact sports.

Etymology[edit]

The origin of the word nunchaku (ヌンチャク) is not known. Another name for this weapon is "nūchiku"(ヌウチク).[8]

In the English language, nunchaku are often referred to as "nunchuks".[9]

Origins

Hyoshiki (wooden clappers)

A South-East Asian rice threshing tool similar in design to nunchaku.

The origin of the nunchaku is unclear, although one popular belief is that nunchaku was originally a short South-East Asian flail. A near identical weapon to the nunchaku called tabak-toyok exists in the northern Philippines,[10] which was used to thresh rice or soybeans. Alternative theories are that it was originally developed from an Okinawan horse bit (muge) or from a wooden clapper called hyoshiki[11] carried by the village night watch, made of two blocks of wood joined by a cord. The night watch would hit the blocks of wood together to attract people's attention, then warn them about fires and other dangers.[12]

The suggestion that nunchaku and other Okinawan weapons were developed and used by rebellious peasants is most likely a romantic exaggeration. Martial arts in Okinawa were practiced exclusively by aristocracy (kazoku) and "serving nobles" (shizoku), but were prohibited among commoners (heimin).[13] According to Chinese folklore, nunchaku are a variation of the two section staff.[14]

Parts

Parts of nunchaku

Ana: the hole on the kontoh of each handle for the himo to pass through—only nunchaku that are connected by himo have an ana.

Himo: the rope which connects the two handles of some nunchaku.

Kusari: the chain which connects the two handles of some nunchaku.

Kontoh: the top of each handle.

Jukon-bu: the upper area of the handle.

Chukon-bu: the center part of the handle.

Kikon-bu: the lower part of the handle.

Kontei: the bottom of the handle.[15]

Construction

Close-up image of the kontoh (top) of two nunchaku, showing the kusari (chain) on one, and the himo (rope) and ana (hole) that the himo goes through on the other.

Uncommon nunchuks made of solid nylon, hollow aluminum, and solid metal (unlinked)

Nunchaku consist of two sections of wood connected by a cord or chain, though variants may include additional sections of wood and chain. In China, the striking stick is called "dragon stick" ("龍棍"), while the handle is called "yang stick" ("陽棍"). Most nunchaku tend to have rounded sticks, whereas others have an octagonal cross-section based on the appearance of sticks made with traditional wood-working techniques. (Making a rounded stick with hand tools would have been much more difficult.) Ideally, each piece should be long enough to protect the forearm when held in a high grip near the top of the shaft. Both ends are usually of equal length, although asymmetrical nunchaku exist that are closer to a traditional flail.

The ideal length of the connecting rope or chain is just long enough to allow the user to lay it over his or her palm, with the sticks hanging comfortably and perpendicular to the ground. The weapon should be properly balanced in terms of weight. Cheaper or gimmicky nunchaku (such as glow-in-the-dark versions) are often not properly balanced, which prevents the performer from performing the more advanced and flashier "low-grip" moves, such as overhand twirls. The weight should be balanced towards the outer edges of the sticks for maximum ease and control of the swing arcs.

Traditional nunchaku are made from a strong, flexible hardwood such as oak, loquat or pasania.

Formal styles

The nunchaku is most commonly used in Okinawan kobudō and karate, but it is also used in Korean hapkido and eskrima. (More accurately, the Tabak-Toyok, a similar though distinct Philippine weapon, is used, not the Okinawan nunchaku). Its application is different in each style. The traditional Okinawan forms use the sticks primarily to grip and lock. Filipino martial artists use it much the same way they would wield a stick: striking is given precedence. Korean systems combine offensive and defensive moves, so both locks and strikes are taught. Other proprietary systems of Nunchaku are also used in Sembkalah (Iranian Monolingual Combat Style), which makes lethal blows in defense and assault.

Nunchaku is often the first weapon wielded by a student, to teach self-restraint and posture, as the weapon is liable to hit the wielder more than the opponent if not used properly.

The Nunchaku is usually wielded in one hand, but it can also be dual wielded. It can be whirled around, using its hardened handles for blunt force, as well as wrapping its chain around an attacking weapon to immobilize or disarm an opponent. Nunchaku training has been noted[by whom?] to increase hand speed, improve posture, and condition the hands of the practitioner. Therefore, it makes a useful training weapon.

Freestyle

Freestyle nunchaku is a modern style of performance art using nunchaku as a visual tool, rather than as a weapon. With the growing prevalence of the Internet, the availability of nunchaku has greatly increased. In combination with the popularity of other video sharing sites, many people have become interested in learning how to use the weapons for freestyle displays. Freestyle is one discipline of competition held by the World Nunchaku Association. Some modern martial arts teach the use of nunchaku, as it may help students improve their reflexes, hand control, and other skills.

Sporting associations

This section relies too much on references to primary sources. Please improve this section by adding secondary or tertiary sources. (December 2020) (Learn how and when to remove this template message)

Since the 1980s, there have been various international sporting associations that organize the use of nunchaku as a contact sport.[16][17] Current associations usually hold "semi-contact" fights, where severe strikes are prohibited, as opposed to "contact" fights. "Full-Nunch" matches, on the other hand, are limitation-free on the severity of strikes and knockout is permissible.[18]

American Style Nunchaku Federation (ASNF): Founded by Grand Master Michael Burke in 1992 and focuses tournament forms and Katas.

North American Nunchaku Association (NANA): Founded in 2003 in California by Sensei Chris Pellitteri, NANA teaches all aspects of the nunchaku, traditional and free-style, single and double.

World Amateur Nunchaku Organization (WANO): Founded by Pascal Verhille in France in 1988.

Fédération Internationale de Nunchaku de Combat et Artistique (FINCA): Founded by Raphaël Schmitz in France in 1992 as a merger of disbanded associations WANO and FFNS (Fédération Française de Nunchaku Sportif). Its current name is Fédération Internationale de Nunchaku, Combat complet et Arts martiaux modernes et affinitaires (FINCA).[19] A fight with FINCA rules lasts two rounds of two minutes. There is no need for changing either the nunchaku branch or the hand before hitting, just a correct recuperation. There are no stops during the fight, except for loss, lifting, or penalties.

World Nunchaku Association (WNA): Founded by Milco Lambrecht in the Netherlands in 1996.[20] WNA uses yellow and black plastic weight-balanced training nunchaku and protective headgear. They have their own belt color system, in which participants earn color stripes on the belt, instead of fully colored belts. One side of the belt is yellow and the other black, so that in a competition, opponents may be distinguished by the visible side of the belt. WNA fight rules correspond to the kumite subsection of Nunchaku-do discipline.[21] It is a two-minutes "touch fight," in which technical abilities are very important. After each scored point, the fight stops and the fighters take back their starting position.

International Techdo Nunchaku Association (ITNA): Founded by Daniel Althaus in Switzerland in 2006. ITNA rules fights last two rounds lasting 2:30. There are no stops during the round, except for loss, lifting, or penalties. Between two strikes, the fighter has to change hand and nunchaku branch before hitting again, except if he blocks.

Nunchaku-en-Savate (ARSIC-International): First presented by Jean-Noel Eynard, Professeur of Savate, pioneer of FFBFSDA Savate in the USA. The sport combines technique of Savate with Nunchaku similar to Savate combined with la Canne. Nunchaku-en-savate rebirth occurred in the Ivory-Coast in the late 1970s. It was taught in classes of Self Defense Savate. The sport made its way to the USA in 1983.

Legality

In a number of countries, possession of nunchaku is illegal, or the nunchaku is defined as a regulated weapon. These bans largely came after the wave of popularity of Bruce Lee films, when nunchaku were believed to be extraordinarily dangerous. Norway, Canada,[22][23] Russia, Poland, Chile, and Spain are all known to have significant restrictions.

In Germany, nunchaku have been illegal since April 2006, when they were declared a strangling weapon.[24][25]

In England and Wales, public possession of nunchaku is heavily restricted by the Prevention of Crime Act 1953 and the Criminal Justice Act 1988. However, nunchaku are not included in the list of weapons whose sale and manufacture is prohibited by Schedule 1 of the Criminal Justice Act 1988

(Offensive Weapons) Order 1988 and are traded openly (subject to age restrictions).

In Scotland, laws restricting offensive weapons are similar to those of England and Wales. However, in a case in 2010, Glasgow Sheriff Court refused to accept a defence submission that nunchaku were not explicitly prohibited weapons under Scottish law, although the defendants were acquitted on other grounds.[26]

The use of nunchaku was, in the 1990s, censored from UK rebroadcasts of American children's TV shows such as Teenage Mutant Ninja Turtles cartoons and films.[27] The UK version of the Soul Blade video game was also edited, replacing the character Li Long's nunchaku with a three-sectioned staff.

In Hong Kong, it is illegal to possess metal or wooden nunchaku connected by a chain, though one can obtain a license from the police as a martial arts instructor, and rubber nunchaku are still allowed. Possession of nunchaku in mainland China is legal.

Australia varies by state laws. In New South Wales, the weapon is on the restricted weapons list and, thus, can only be owned with a permit.

The United States varies at the state level. As elsewhere, the popularity of Bruce Lee movies in the 1970s led to a wave of nunchaku bans.[28] Many states prohibit carrying nunchaku in public as a concealed weapon, but a small number restrict or completely ban ownership. California has made exceptions for professional martial arts schools and practitioners to use the nunchaku.[29] The state of Arizona previously considered nunchaku to be a "prohibited weapon" since the 1970s, making mere possession illegal, with the sole exception of nunchaku-like objects that are manufactured for use as illumination devices.[30] A constitutional challenge failed as well.[31] It was legalized in 2019.[28] New York formerly banned all possession of nunchaku, but this was ruled unconstitutional in the 2018 case Maloney v. Singas.[32]

Law enforcement use

Nunchaku have been employed by a few American police departments for decades, especially after the popular Bruce Lee movies of the 1970's. For instance, in 2015, police in the small town of Anderson, California were trained and deployed to use nunchaku as a form of non-lethal force.[33] They were selected because of their utility as both a striking weapon and a control tool.

Orcutt Police Nunchaku (OPN) had been adopted by more than 200 law enforcement agencies in the USA. Even though it could be used as a striking weapon, it was mainly used as a grappling implement on the wrists and ankles for pain compliance. They were very effective in that regard but improper use had been associated with injuries like wrist and limb breaks that led to them being phased out.[34]

However, tasers have become the preferred non-lethal weapon for

CHAPTER EIGHT

Kunai

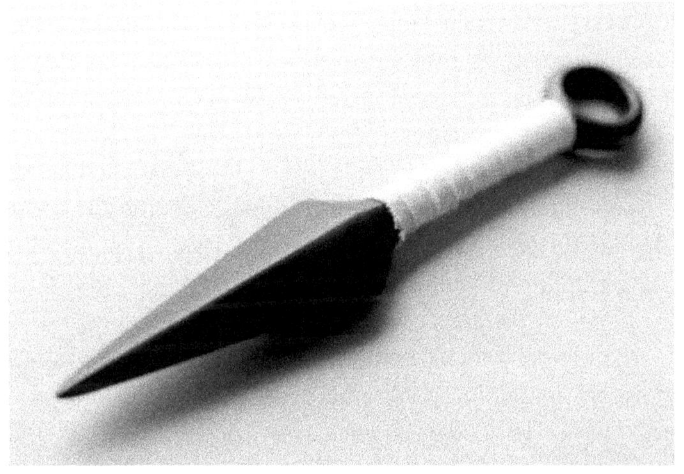

Kunai

A kunai (苦無, kunai) is a Japanese tool thought to be originally derived from the masonry trowel.[1] The two widely recognized variations of the kunai are short kunai (小苦無 shō-kunai) and the big kunai (大苦無 dai-kunai). Although a basic tool, in the hands of a martial arts expert, the kunai could be used as a multi-functional weapon. The kunai is commonly associated with the ninja, who used it to gouge holes in walls.

Design

A Kunai normally had a leaf-shaped wrought blade in lengths ranging from 20 cm to 30 cm and a handle with a ring on the pommel for attaching a rope. The attached rope allowed the kunai's handle to be wrapped to function as a grip, or to be strapped to a stick as a makeshift spear; to be tied to the body for concealment; to be used as an anchor or piton, and sometimes to be used as the Chinese rope dart. Contrary to popular belief, kunai were not designed to be used primarily as throwing weapons. Instead, kunai were primarily tools and, when used as weapons, were stabbing and thrusting implements.

Varieties of kunai include short, long, narrow-bladed, saw-toothed, and wide-bladed. In some cases, the kunai and the shikoro, a wide-bladed saw with a dagger-type handle, are difficult to distinguish.

Uses

The kunai was originally used by peasants as a multi-purpose gardening tool and by workers of stone and masonry. The blade is made of soft iron, and is left unsharpened because the edges are used to smash relatively soft materials such as plaster and wood, for digging holes and for prying. Normally, only the tip is sharpened.

Weapon

Many ninja weapons were adapted from farming tools, not unlike those used by Shaolin monks in China. Since kunai were cheaply produced farming tools of a useful size and weight and could be easily sharpened, they were readily available to be converted into simple weapons.[citation needed] As a weapon, the kunai is larger and heavier than a shuriken and with the grip could also be used in hand-to-hand combat more readily than a shuriken.[citation needed]

As with ninjutsu, the exaggeration persistent in ninja myths played a large role in creating the popular culture image of kunai. In fictional depictions of ninjas, the kunai is commonly portrayed as a steel knife that is used for stabbing or particularly throwing, sometimes confusing it with the shuriken.[citation needed]

Masonry

The kunai was used in masonry to shape stonework.

CHAPTER NINE

Crossbow

Crossbow

A crossbow is a ranged weapon using an elastic launching device consisting of a bow-like assembly called a prod, mounted horizontally on a main frame called a tiller, which is hand-held in a similar fashion to the stock of a long firearm. Crossbows shoot arrow-like projectiles called bolts or quarrels. A person who shoots crossbow is called a crossbowman or an arbalist (after the arbalest, a European crossbow variant used during the 12th century).[1]

Although crossbows and bows use the same launch principle, the difference is that an archer must maintain a bow's draw manually by pitching the bowstring with fingers, pulling it back with arm and back muscles and then holding that same form in order to aim (which distresses the body and demands significant physical strength and stamina); while a crossbow utilizes a locking mechanism to maintain the draw, limiting the shooter's exertion to only pulling the string into lock and then releasing the shot via depressing a lever/trigger. This not only enables a crossbowman to handle stronger draw weight, but also to hold for longer with significantly less physical strain, thus potentially achieving better precision.

Historically, crossbows played a significant role in the warfare of East Asia and Europe.[2] The earliest known crossbows were invented in the first millennium BC, not later than the 7th century BC in ancient China, not later than the 1st century AD in Greece (as the gastraphetes). Crossbows brought about a major shift in the role of projectile weaponry in wars, such as during Qin's unification wars and later the Han campaigns against northern nomads and western states. The medieval European crossbow was called by many names, including "crossbow" itself; most of these names derived from the word ballista, an ancient Greek torsion siege engine similar in appearance but different in design principle.[3] The traditional bow and arrow had long been a specialized weapon that required considerable training, physical strength, and expertise to operate with any degree of practical efficiency. Many cultures treated archers as a separate and superior warrior caste, despite usually being drawn from the common class, as their archery skill-set was essentially trained and strengthened from early childhood (similar to many cavalry-oriented cultures) and was impossible to reproduce outside a pre-established cultural tradition, which many cultures lacked. In contrast, the crossbow was the first ranged weapon to be simple, cheap and physically undemanding enough to be operated by large numbers of untrained conscript soldiers, thus enabling virtually any military body to field a potent force of crossbowmen with little expense beyond the cost of the weapons themselves.[4]

In modern times, firearms have largely supplanted bows and crossbows as weapons of warfare. However, crossbows still remain widely used for competitive shooting sports and hunting, or for relatively silent shooting.[5]

It is possible to turn at least some store-bought bows into a crossbow. It is done by marrying a stock-and-trigger system to a bow.[6]

Terminology

A crossbowman or crossbow-maker is sometimes called an arbalista, arbalist or arbalest. The latter two are also used to refer to the crossbow.[7]

Arrow, bolt and quarrel are all suitable terms for crossbow projectiles.[1]

The lath, also called the prod, is the bow of the crossbow. According to W.F. Peterson, the prod came into usage in the 19th century as a result of mistranslating rodd in a 16th-century list of crossbow effects.[1]

The stock is the wooden body on which the bow is mounted, although the medieval tiller is also used.[1]

The lock refers to the release mechanism, including the string, sears, trigger lever, and housing.[1]

Construction

Han dynasty crossbow trigger pieces.

Crossbow nut:

Nut.

String.

Quarrel.

Trigger.

A 16th century crossbow nut was excavated at Harburger Schloßstraße, Hamburg Harburg, Germany

A crossbow is essentially a bow mounted on an elongated frame (called a tiller or stock) with a built-in mechanism that holds the drawn bow string, as well as a trigger mechanism that allows the string to be released.

Chinese vertical trigger lock

The nu (弩) [crossbow] is so called because it spreads abroad an aura of rage [nù] (怒) . Its stock is like the arm of a man, therefore it is called bi (臂). That which hooks the bowstring is called ya (牙), for indeed it is like teeth. The part round about the teeth [i.e. the housing box] is called the guo (郭) ["city wall"], since it surrounds the gui (規) [lug] of the teeth [i.e. the locking nut]. Within [and below] there is the xuan dao (懸刀) ["hanging knife", i.e. the trigger blade] so called because it looks like one. The whole assembly is called ji (機)["machine" or "mechanism"], for it is just as ingenious as the loom.[8]

— Shiming

The Chinese trigger was a complex mechanism typically composed of three cast bronze pieces housed inside a hollow bronze enclosure. The entire mechanism is then dropped into a carved slot within the tiller and secured together by two bronze rods.[1] The string catch (nut) is shaped like a "J" because it usually have a tall erect rear spine that protrudes above the housing, which serves the function of both a cocking lever (by pushing the drawn string onto it) and a primitive rear sight. It is held stationary against tension by the second piece, which is shaped like a flattened "C" and acts as the sear. The sear cannot move as it is trapped by the third piece, i.e. the actual trigger blade, which hangs vertically below the enclosure and catches the sear via a notch. The two bearing surfaces between the three trigger pieces each offers a mechanical advantage, which allow for handling significant draw weights with a much smaller pull weight. During shooting, the user will hold the crossbow at eye level by a vertical handle and aim along the arrow using the sighting spine for elevation, similar to how a modern rifleman shoots with iron sights. When the trigger blade is pulled, its notch disengages from the sear and allows the latter to drop downwards, which in turn frees up the nuts to pivot forward and release the bowstring.

European rolling nut lock

The earliest European designs featured a transverse slot in the top surface of the frame, down into which the string was placed. To shoot this design, a vertical rod is thrust up through a hole in the bottom of the notch, forcing the string out. This rod is usually attached perpendicular to a rear-facing lever called a tickler. A later design implemented a rolling cylindrical pawl called a nut to retain the string. This nut has a perpendicular centre slot for the bolt, and an intersecting axial slot for the string, along with a lower face or slot against which the internal trigger sits. They often also have some form of strengthening internal sear or trigger face, usually of metal. These roller nuts were either free-floating in their close-fitting hole across the stock, tied in with a binding of sinew or other strong cording; or mounted on a metal axle or pins. Removable or integral plates of wood, ivory, or metal on the sides of the stock kept the nut in place laterally. Nuts were made of antler, bone, or metal. Bows could be kept taut and ready to shoot for some time with little physical straining, allowing crossbowmen to aim better without fatiguing.[9]

Bow

Chinese crossbow bows were made of composite material from the start.[1]

European crossbows from the 10th to 12th centuries used wood for the bow, also called the prod or lath, which tended to be ash or yew.[1]

Composite bows started appearing in Europe during the 13th century and could be made from layers of different material, often wood, horn, and sinew glued together and bound with animal tendon. These composite bows made of several layers are much stronger and more efficient in releasing energy than simple wooden bows.[1]

The Chinese used winches for large crossbows mounted on fortifications or wagons, known as "bedded crossbows" (床弩). Winches may have been used for handheld crossbows during the Han dynasty, but there is only one known depiction of it. The Wujing Zongyao mentions types of crossbows using winch mechanisms, but it is not known if these were actually handheld crossbows or mounted crossbows.[10] Another drawing method involved the shooters sitting on the ground, and using the combined strength of leg, waist, back and arm muscles to help span much heavier crossbows, which were aptly called "waist-spun crossbows" (腰張弩).

During the Medieval period, both Chinese and European crossbows used stirrups as well as belt hooks.[10] In the 13th century European crossbows started using winches, and from the 14th century an assortment of spanning mechanisms such as winch pulleys, cord pulleys, gaffles (such as gaffe levers, goat's foot levers, and rarer internal lever-action mechanisms), cranequins, and even screws.[1][11]

Battle scene depicting a man spanning a crossbow using a winch mechanism, possibly mounted on a frame, Han dynasty

Song dynasty cavalry wielding crossbows with stirrups

Fifteenth century crossbowman using a stirrup along with a belt hook and pulley

Detailed illustration of a goat's foot lever mounted on a crossbow that is half-spanned

Illustration of a gaffe lever mounted on a crossbow that is nearly at full-span.

Illustrations of Leonardo da Vinci's rapid fire crossbow in the 15th Century Codex Atlanticus. Note the internal lever mechanism is fully extended to catch the draw string.

Internal mechanics illustration of a Balester hunting crossbow's self-spanning mechanism

Twentieth century depiction of a windlass pulley

Fifteenth century crossbowman using a cranequin (rack & pinion)

Iron cranequin, South German, late 15th century

Variants

Modern recurve crossbow

Modern compound crossbow

15th-century Wallarmbrust, a heavy crossbow used for siege defense.

The smallest crossbows are pistol crossbows. Others are simple long stocks with the crossbow mounted on them. These could be shot from under the arm. The next step in development was stocks of the shape that would later be used for firearms, which allowed better aiming. The arbalest was a heavy crossbow that required special systems for pulling the sinew via windlasses. For siege warfare, the size of crossbows was further increased to hurl large projectiles, such as rocks, at fortifications. The required crossbows needed a massive base frame and powerful windlass devices.[12]

Double shot repeating crossbow, also known as the Chu state repeating crossbow (chuguo nu)

Mounted double bow crossbow

Mounted triple bow crossbow

Multi-bolt crossbow without a visible nut or cocking aid

Cocking of a Greek gastraphetes

Gallo-Roman crossbow

Earliest European depiction of cavalry using crossbows, from the Catalan manuscript Four Horsemen of the Apocalypse, 1086.

Late medieval crossbowman from ca. 1480

15th-century French soldier carrying an arbalest and a pavise

A reconstruction of Leonardo da Vinci's rapid fire crossbow as shown at the World of Leonardo Exhibition in Milan.

Early modern four-wheeled ballista drawn by armored horses (1552)

16th-century French mounted crossbowman (cranequinier). His crossbow is drawn with a rack-and-pinion cranequin, so it can be used while riding.

Pistol crossbow for home recreational shooting. Made by Frédéric Siber in Morges, early 19th century, on display at Morges military museum.

French cross-bow grenade thrower Arbalète sauterelle type A d'Imphy, circa 1915

Projectiles

Arrowheads and lead balls, Han dynasty

The arrow-like projectiles of a crossbow are called crossbow bolts. These are usually much shorter than arrows, but can be several times heavier. There is an optimum weight for bolts to achieve maximum kinetic energy, which varies depending on the strength and characteristics of the crossbow, but most could pass through common mail. Crossbow bolts can be fitted with a variety of heads, some with sickle-shaped heads to cut rope or rigging; but the most common today is a four-sided point called a quarrel. A highly specialized type of bolt is employed to collect blubber biopsy samples used in biology research.

Even relatively small differences in arrow weight can have a considerable impact on its drop and, conversely, its flight trajectory.[13]

Accessories

The reticle of a modern crossbow telescopic sight allows the shooter to adjust for different ranges

The ancient Chinese crossbow often included a metal (i.e. bronze or steel) grid serving as iron sights. Modern crossbow sights often use similar technology to modern firearm sights, such as red dot sights and telescopic sights. Many crossbow scopes feature multiple crosshairs to compensate for the significant effects of gravity over different ranges. In most cases, a newly bought crossbow will need to be sighted for accurate shooting.[14]

A major cause of the sound of shooting a crossbow is vibration of various components. Crossbow silencers are multiple components placed on high vibration parts, such as the string and limbs, to dampen vibration and suppress the sound of loosing the bolt.[15]

History

Main article: History of crossbows

China

A bronze crossbow trigger mechanism and butt plate that were mass-produced in the Warring States period (475–221 BC)

A miniature guard wielding a handheld crossbow from the top balcony of a model watchtower, made of glazed earthenware during the Eastern Han era (25–220 AD) of China, from the Metropolitan Museum of Art.

In terms of archaeological evidence, crossbow locks made of cast bronze have been found in China dating to around 650 BC.[1] They have also been found in Tombs 3 and 12 at Qufu, Shandong, previously the capital of Lu, and date to the 6th century BC.[16][17] Bronze crossbow bolts dating from the mid-5th century BC have been found at a Chu burial site in Yutaishan, Jiangling County, Hubei Province.[18] Other early finds of crossbows were discovered in Tomb 138 at Saobatang, Hunan Province, and date to the mid-4th century BC.[19][20] It is possible that these early crossbows used spherical pellets for ammunition. A Western-Han mathematician and music theorist, Jing Fang (78–37 BC), compared the moon to the shape of a round crossbow bullet.[21] The Zhuangzi also mentions crossbow bullets.[22]

The earliest Chinese documents mentioning a crossbow were texts from the 4th to 3rd centuries BC attributed to the followers of Mozi. This source refers to the use of a giant crossbow between the 6th and 5th centuries BC, corresponding to the late Spring and Autumn Period. Sun Tzu's The Art of War (first appearance dated between 500

BC to 300 BC[23]) refers to the characteristics and use of crossbows in chapters 5 and 12 respectively,[24] and compares a drawn crossbow to "might".[25] The Huainanzi advises its readers not to use crossbows in marshland where the surface is soft and it is hard to arm the crossbow with the foot.[26] The Records of the Grand Historian, completed in 94 BC, mentions that Sun Bin defeated Pang Juan by ambushing him with a body of crossbowmen at the Battle of Maling in 342 BC.[27] The Book of Han, finished 111 AD, lists two military treatises on crossbows.[28][29]

Handheld crossbows with complex bronze trigger mechanisms have also been found with the Terracotta Army in the tomb of Qin Shihuang (r. 221–210 BC) that are similar to specimens from the subsequent Han Dynasty (202 BC–220 AD), while crossbowmen described in the Qin and Han Dynasty learned drill formations, some were even mounted as charioteers and cavalry units, and Han Dynasty writers attributed the success of numerous battles against the Xiongnu and Western Regions city-states to massed crossbow volleys.[30][31] The bronze triggers were designed in such a way that they were able to store a large amount of energy within the bow when drawn, but was easily shot with little resistance and recoil when the trigger were pulled. The trigger nut also had a long vertical spine that could be used like a primitive rear sight for elevation adjustment, which allowed precision shooting over longer distances. The Qin/Han-era crossbow was also an early example of modular design, as the bronze trigger components were also mass-produced with relative precise tolerances so that the parts are interchangeable between different crossbows. The trigger mechanism from one crossbow can be installed into another simply by dropping into a tiller slot of the same specifications and secured with dowel pins. Some crossbow designs were also found to be fitted with bronze buttplates and trigger guard.

It is clear from surviving inventory lists in Gansu and Xinjiang that the crossbow was greatly favored by the Han dynasty. For example, in one batch of slips there are only two mentions of bows, but thirty mentions of crossbows.[26] Crossbows were mass-produced in state armories with designs improving as time went on, such as the use of a mulberry wood stock and brass; a crossbow in 1068 could pierce a tree at 140 paces.[32] Crossbows were used in numbers as large as 50,000 starting from the Qin dynasty and upwards of several hundred thousand during the Han.[33] According to one authority, the crossbow had become "nothing less than the standard weapon of the Han armies", by the second century BC.[34] Han soldiers were required to pull a crossbow with a draw weight equivalent of 76 kg (168 pounds) to qualify as an entry level crossbowman,[1] while it was claimed that a few elite troops were capable of bending crossbows by the hands-and-feet method, with a draw-weight in excess of 750lb.[35][36]

After the Han dynasty, the crossbow lost favor during the Six Dynasties until it experienced a mild resurgence during the Tang dynasty, under which the ideal expeditionary army of 20,000 included 2,200 archers and 2,000 crossbowmen.[37] Li Jing and Li Quan prescribed 20 percent of the infantry to be armed with crossbows.[38]

During the Song dynasty, the crossbow received a huge upsurge in military usage, and often overshadowed the bow 2 to 1 in numbers. During this time period, a stirrup was added for ease of loading. The Song government attempted to restrict the public use of crossbows and sought ways to keep both body armors and crossbows out of civilian ownership.[39] Despite the ban on certain types of crossbows, the weapon experienced an upsurge in civilian usage as both a hunting weapon and pastime. The "romantic young people from rich families, and others who had nothing particular to do" formed crossbow shooting clubs as a way to pass time.[40]

During the late Ming dynasty, no crossbows were mentioned to have been produced in the three-year period from 1619 to 1622. With 21,188,366 taels, the Ming manufactured 25,134 cannons, 8,252 small guns, 6,425 muskets, 4,090 culverins, 98,547 polearms and swords, 26,214 great "horse decapitator" swords, 42,800 bows, 1,000 great axes, 2,284,000 arrows, 180,000 fire arrows, 64,000 bow strings, and hundreds of transport carts.[41]

Military crossbows were armed by treading, or basically placing the feet on the bow stave and drawing it using one's arms and back muscles. During the Song dynasty, stirrups were added for ease of drawing and to mitigate damage to the bow. Alternatively the bow could also be drawn by a belt claw attached to the waist, but this was done lying down, as was the case for all large crossbows. Winch-drawing was used for the large mounted crossbows as seen below, but evidence for its use in Chinese hand-crossbows is scant.[10]

Other sorts of crossbows also existed, such as the repeating crossbow, multi-shot crossbow, larger field artillery crossbows, and repeating multi-shot crossbow.

Southeast Asia

Wheelmounted and elephantmounted double-bow-arcuballistae in the Khmer army, possibly Cham mercenaries

In Vietnamese historical legend, general Thục Phán, who ruled over the ancient kingdom of Âu Lạc from 257 to 207 BC, is said to have owed his power to a magic crossbow, capable of shooting thousands of bolts at once.

The native Montagnards of Vietnam's Central Highlands were also known to have used crossbows, as both a tool for hunting, and later, an effective weapon against the Viet Cong during the Vietnam War.[42] Montagnard fighters armed with crossbows proved a highly valuable asset to the US Special Forces operating in Vietnam, and it was not uncommon for the Green Berets to integrate Montagnard crossbowmen into their strike teams.[43]

Crossbow technology for crossbows with more than one prod was transferred from the Chinese to Champa, which Champa used in its invasion of the Khmer Empire's Angkor in 1177.[44] When the Chams sacked Angkor they used the Chinese siege crossbow.[45][46] Crossbows and archery while mounted were instructed to the Cham by a Chinese in 1171.[47] The Khmer also had double bow crossbows mounted on elephants, which Michel Jacq-Hergoualc'h suggests were elements of Cham mercenaries in Jayavarman VII's army.[48]

Ancient Greece

Greek gastraphetes

The earliest crossbow-like weapons in Europe probably emerged around the late 5th century BC when the gastraphetes, an ancient Greek crossbow, appeared. The device was described by the Greek author Heron of Alexandria in his Belopoeica ("On Catapult-making"), which draws on an earlier account of his compatriot engineer Ctesibius (fl. 285–222 BC). According to Heron, the gastraphetes was the forerunner of the later catapult, which places its invention some unknown time prior to 399 BC.[49] The gastraphetes was a crossbow mounted on a stock divided into a lower and upper section. The lower was a case fixed to the bow while the upper was a slider which had the same dimensions as the case.[50] Meaning "belly-bow",[50] it was called as such because the concave withdrawal rest at one end of the stock was placed against the stomach of the operator, which he could press to withdraw the slider before attaching a string to the trigger and loading the bolt; this could thus store more energy than regular Greek bows.[51] It was used in the Siege of Motya in 397 BC. This was a key Carthaginian stronghold in Sicily, as described in the 1st century AD by Heron of Alexandria in his book Belopoeica.[52]

Other arrow shooting machines such as the larger ballista and smaller Scorpio also existed starting from around 338 BC, but these are torsion catapults and not considered crossbows.[53][54][55] Arrow-shooting machines (katapeltai) are briefly mentioned by Aeneas Tacticus in his treatise on siegecraft written around 350 BC.[53] An Athenian inventory from 330–329 BC includes catapults bolts with heads and flights.[55] Arrow-shooting machines in action are reported from Philip II's siege of Perinthos in Thrace in 340 BC.[56] At the same time, Greek fortifications began to feature high towers with shuttered windows in the top, presumably to house anti-personnel arrow shooters, as in Aigosthena.[57]

Ancient Rome

A crossbow based on depictions from a Roman grave in Gaul.

The late 4th century author Vegetius provides the only contemporary account of ancient Roman crossbows. In his De Re Militaris, he describes arcubalistarii (crossbowmen) working together with archers and artillerymen.[1] However it is disputed if arcuballistas were crossbows or torsion powered weapons. The idea that the arcuballista was a crossbow is based on the fact that Vegetius refers to it and the manuballista, which was torsion powered, separately. Therefore, if the arcuballista was not like the manuballista, it may have been a crossbow. The etymology is not clear and their definitions obscure. According to Vegetius, these were well-known devices, and hence he did not describe them in depth.[58]

On the textual side, there is almost nothing but passing references in the military historian Vegetius (fl. + 386) to 'manuballistae' and 'arcuballistae' which he said he must decline to describe as they were so well known. His decision was highly regrettable, as no other author of the time makes any mention of them at all. Perhaps the best supposition is that the crossbow was primarily known in late European antiquity as a hunting weapon, and received only local use in certain units of the armies of Theodosius I, with which Vegetius happened to be acquainted.[58]

— Joseph Needham

Arrian's earlier Ars Tactica, written around 136 AD, does mention 'missiles shot not from a bow but from a machine' and that this machine was used on horseback while in full gallop. It is presumed that this was a crossbow.[1]

The only pictorial evidence of Roman arcuballistas comes from sculptural reliefs in Roman Gaul depicting them in hunting scenes. These are aesthetically similar to both the Greek and Chinese crossbows, but it's not clear what kind of release mechanism they used. Archaeological evidence suggests they were based on the rolling nut mechanism of medieval Europe.[1]

Medieval Europe

A medieval crossbowman drawing his bow behind his pavise. A hook on the end of a strap on his belt engages the bowstring. Holding the crossbow down by putting his foot through the stirrup, he draws the bow by straightening his legs

References to the crossbow are basically nonexistent in Europe from the 5th century until the 10th century. There is however a depiction of a crossbow as a hunting weapon on four Pictish stones from early medieval Scotland (6th to 9th centuries): St. Vigeans no. 1, Glenferness, Shandwick, and Meigle.[59]

The crossbow reappeared again in 947 as a French weapon during the siege of Senlis and again in 984 at the siege of Verdun.[60] Crossbows were used at the battle of Hastings in 1066 and by the 12th century they had become common battlefield weapons.[61] The earliest extant European crossbow remains to date were found at Lake Paladru and has been dated to the 11th century.[1]

The crossbow superseded hand bows in many European armies during the 12th century, except in England, where the longbow was more popular. Later crossbows (sometimes referred to as arbalests), utilizing all-steel prods, were able to achieve power close (and sometime superior) to longbows, but were more expensive to produce and slower to reload because they required the aid of mechanical devices such as the cranequin or windlass to draw back their extremely heavy bows. Usually these could only shoot two bolts per minute versus twelve or more with a skilled archer, often necessitating the use of a pavise to protect the operator from enemy fire.[62] Along with polearm weapons made from farming equipment, the crossbow was also a weapon of choice for insurgent peasants such as the Taborites. Genoese crossbowmen were famous mercenaries hired throughout medieval Europe, while the crossbow also played an important role in anti-personnel defense of ships.[63]

Sketch by Leonardo da Vinci, c. 1500

Crossbows were eventually replaced in warfare by gunpowder weapons. Early hand cannons had slower rates of fire and much worse accuracy than contemporary crossbows, but the arquebus (which proliferated in the mid to late 15th century) matched their rate of fire while being far more powerful. The Battle of Cerignola in 1503 was largely won by Spain through the use of matchlock arquebuses, marking the first time a major battle was won through the use of hand-held firearms. Later, similar competing tactics would feature harquebusiers or musketeers in formation with pikemen, pitted against cavalry firing pistols or carbines. While the military crossbow had largely been supplanted by firearms on the battlefield by 1525, the sporting crossbow in various forms remained a popular hunting weapon in Europe until the eighteenth century.[64] Crossbows saw irregular use throughout the rest of the 16th century; for example, Maria Pita's husband was killed by a crossbowman of the English Armada in 1589.

Islamic world

There are no references to crossbows in Islamic texts earlier than the 14th century. Arabs in general were averse to the crossbow and considered it a foreign weapon. They called it qaus al-rijl (foot-drawn bow), qaus al-zanbūrak (bolt bow) and qaus al-faranjīyah (Frankish bow). Although Muslims did have crossbows, there seems to be a split between eastern and western types. Muslims in Spain used the typical European trigger while eastern Muslim crossbows had a more complex trigger mechanism.[65]

Mamluk cavalry used crossbows.[1]

Elsewhere

In Western Africa and Central Africa,[66] crossbows served as a scouting weapon and for hunting, with African slaves bringing this technology to natives in America.[67] In the US South, the crossbow was used for hunting and warfare when firearms or gunpowder were unavailable because of economic hardships or isolation.[67] In the North of Northern America, light hunting crossbows were traditionally used by the Inuit.[68][non-tertiary source needed] These are technologically similar to the African derived crossbows, but have a different route of influence.

Spanish conquistadors continued to use crossbows in the Americas long after they were replaced in European battlefields by firearms. Only in the 1570s did firearms became completely dominant among the Spanish in the Americas.[69]

The French and the British used a Sauterelle (French for grasshopper) in World War I. It was lighter and more portable than the Leach Trench Catapult, but less powerful. It weighed 24 kg (53 pounds) and could throw an F1 grenade or Mills bomb 110–140 m (120–150 yards).[70] The Sauterelle replaced the Leach Catapult in British service and was in turn replaced in 1916 by the 2-inch Medium Trench Mortar and Stokes mortar.[71]

Modern use

Modern recreation of a mounted triple bow crossbow

Hunting, leisure and science

Main article: Bowhunting

Crossbows are used for shooting sports and bowhunting in modern archery and for blubber biopsy samples in scientific research. In some countries such as Canada or the United Kingdom, they may be less heavily regulated than firearms, and thus more popular for hunting; some jurisdictions have bow and/or crossbow only seasons.[72]

Modern hunting crossbow

Fisheries scientist obtaining tissue samples from dolphins swimming in the bow wave of a NOAA ship

A whale shot by a modified crossbow bolt for a blubber biopsy sample

Modern military and paramilitary use

In modern times, crossbows are no longer used for war, but there are still some applications. For example, in the Americas, the Peruvian army (Ejército) equips some soldiers with crossbows and rope, to establish a zip-line in difficult terrain.[73] In Brazil the CIGS (Jungle Warfare Training Center) also trains soldiers in the use of crossbows.[74] In the United States of America, SAA International Ltd manufacture a 150-foot-pound (200 J) crossbow-launched version of the U.S. Army type classified Launched Grapnel Hook (LGH), among other mine countermeasure solutions designed for the middle-eastern theatre. It has been successfully evaluated in Cambodia and Bosnia.[75] It is used to probe for and detonate tripwire initiated mines and booby traps at up to 50 m (55 yards). The concept is similar to the LGH device originally only fired from a rifle, as a plastic retrieval line is attached.[76] Reusable up to 20 times, the line can be reeled back in without exposing oneself. The device is of particular use in tactical situations where noise discipline is important.[77]

In Europe, Barnett International sold crossbows to Serbian forces which according to The Guardian were later used "in ambushes and as a counter-sniper weapon" against the Kosovo Liberation Army during the Kosovo War in the areas of Pec and Djakovica, south west of Kosovo.[78] Whitehall launched an investigation, though the Department of Trade and Industry established that not being "on the military list", crossbows were not covered by such export regulations. Paul Beaver of Jane's Defence Publications commented that, "They are not only a silent killer, they also have a psychological effect". On 15 February 2008, Serbian Minister of Defence Dragan Sutanovac was pictured testing a Barnett crossbow during a public exercise of the Serbian Army's Special Forces in Nis, 200 km (120 miles) south of capital Belgrade.[79] Special forces in both Greece and Turkey also continue to employ the crossbow.[80][81] Spain's Green Berets still use the crossbow as well.[82]

In Asia, some Chinese armed forces use crossbows, including the special force Snow Leopard Commando Unit of the People's Armed Police and the People's Liberation Army. One justification for this comes in the crossbow's ability to stop persons carrying explosives without risk of causing detonation.[83] During the Xinjiang riots of July 2009, crossbows were used alongside modern military hardware to quell protests.[84] The Indian Navy's Marine Commando Force were equipped until the late 1980s with crossbows supplied with cyanide-tipped bolts, as an alternative to suppressed handguns.[85]

Comparison to conventional bows

With a crossbow, archers could release a draw force far in excess of what they could have handled with a bow. Furthermore, the crossbow could hold the tension for a long time, whereas even the strongest longbowman could only hold a drawn bow for a short period of time. The ease of use of a crossbow allows it to be used effectively with little training, while other types of bows take far more skill to shoot accurately.[86] The disadvantage is the greater weight and clumsiness to reload compared to a bow, as well as the slower rate of shooting and the lower efficiency of the acceleration system, but there would be reduced elastic hysteresis, making the crossbow a more accurate weapon.

Crossbows have a much smaller draw length than bows. This means that for the same energy to be imparted to the arrow (or bolt), the crossbow has to have a much higher draw weight.

A direct comparison between a fast hand-drawn replica crossbow and a longbow show a 6:10 rate of shooting[87] or a 4:9 rate within 30 seconds and comparable weapons.[88]

Legal issues

Main article: Laws on crossbows

Modern competition crossbow

Today, the crossbow often has a complicated legal status due to the possibility of lethal use and its similarities to both firearms and archery weapons. While some jurisdictions regard crossbows the same as firearms, many others do not require any sort of license to own a crossbow. The legality of using a crossbow for hunting varies widely around the world, and even within different jurisdictions of some federal countries.

CHAPTER TEN

Yari

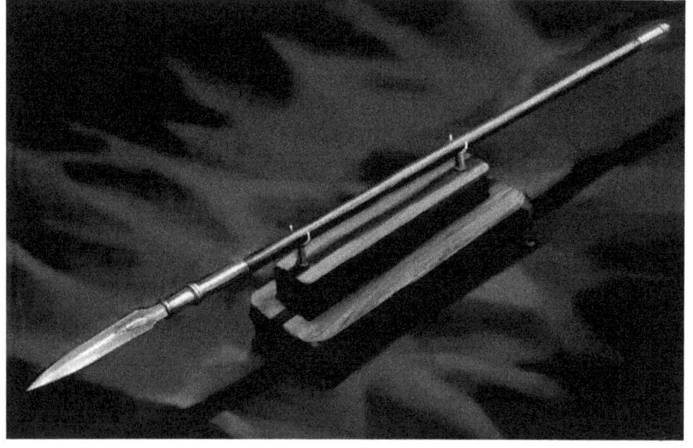

Yari

Yari (槍) is the term for a traditionally-made Japanese blade (nihonto)[2][3] in the form of a spear, or more specifically, the straight-headed spear.[4] The martial art of wielding the yari is called sōjutsu.

History

Ukiyo-e print of a samurai general holding a yari in his right hand

Early yari are believed to have been derived from Chinese spears. These hoko yari are thought to be from the Nara period (710–794).[5][6] While they were present in early Japanese history, the term 'yari' appeared for the first time in written sources in 1334 and this type of spear did not become popular until the late 15th century.[1] The original warfare of the bushi was not a thing for commoners; it was a ritualized combat usually between two warriors who would challenge each other via horseback archery.[7] In the late Heian period, battles on foot began to increase and naginata, a polearm, became a main weapon along with a yumi (longbow).[8] The attempted Mongol invasions of Japan in 1274 and 1281 was one of the factors that changed Japanese weaponry and warfare. The Mongols employed Chinese and Korean footmen wielding long pikes and fought in tight formations. They moved in large units to stave off cavalry.[7] Polearms (including naginata and yari) were of much greater military use than swords, due to their significantly longer reach, lighter weight per unit length (though overall a polearm would be fairly hefty), and their great piercing ability.[7] In the Nanbokuchō period, battles on foot by groups became the mainstream and the importance of naginata further increased, but yari were not yet the main weapon. However, from the Onin War in 15th century in the Muromachi period, large-scale group battles started in which mobilized ashigaru (foot troops) fought on foot and in close quarters, and yari, yumi and tanegashima (Japanese matchlock) became the main weapons.[8][9][10][11] Swords in a full battle situation were therefore relegated to emergency sidearm status from the Heian through the Muromachi periods.[7]

Around the latter half of the 16th century, ashigaru holding pikes (nagae yari) with length of 4.5 to 6.5 m (15 to 21 ft) became the main forces in armies. They formed lines, combined with soldiers bearing firearms tanegashima and short spears. Pikemen formed a two or three row line, and were trained to move their pikes in unison under command. All of The Three Great Spears of Japan were forged by the 16th century in the Muromachi period.[12]

The yari eventually became more popular than the yumi (longbow) as a weapon for the samurai, and foot troops (ashigaru) followed suit and used them extensively.[7] With the coming of the Edo period the yari had fallen into disuse. Greater emphasis was placed on small-scale, close quarters combat, so the convenience of swords led to their dominance, and polearms and archery lost their practical value. During the peaceful Edo period, yari were still produced (sometimes even by renowned swordsmiths), although they existed mostly as either a ceremonial weapon or as a police weapon.

Description

Omi yari (large spear), Tokyo national museum.

Yari were characterized by a straight blade that could be anywhere from several centimeters to 3 feet (0.91 m) or more in length.[4] The blades were made of the same steel (tamahagane) that traditional Japanese swords and arrow heads were forged with, and were very durable.[4] Throughout history many variations of the straight yari blade were produced, often with protrusions on a central blade. Yari blades often had an extremely long tang (nakago); typically it would be longer than the sharpened portion of the blade. The tang protruded into a reinforced hollow portion of the handle (tachiuchi or tachiuke) resulting in a very stiff shaft making it nearly impossible for the blade to fall or break off.[4]

The shaft (nagaye or ebu) came in many different lengths, widths, and shapes; made of hardwood and covered in lacquered bamboo strips, these came in oval, round, or polygonal cross section. These in turn were often wrapped in metal rings or wire (dogane), and affixed with a metal pommel (ishizuki) on the butt end. Yari shafts were often decorated with inlays of metal or semiprecious materials such as brass pins, lacquer, or flakes of pearl. A sheath (saya) was also part of a complete yari.[4]

Variations of yari blades

Straight yari (su yari), detail view; blade is about 1 shaku (approx. 30 cm (12 in) in length)

Various types of yari points or blades existed. The most common blade was a straight, flat design that resembles a straight-bladed double edged dagger.[4] This type of blade could cut as well as stab and was sharpened like a razor edge. Though 'yari' is a catchall term for 'spear', it is usually distinguished between 'kama yari', which have additional horizontal blades, and simple 'su yari' (choku-sō) or straight spears. Yari can also be distinguished by the types of blade cross section: the triangular sections were called 'sankaku yari' and the diamond sections were called 'ryō-shinogi yari'.[4]

Sankaku yari (三角槍, "triangle spear") have a point that resembles a narrow spike with a triangular cross-section. A sankaku yari therefore had no cutting edge, only a sharp point at the end. The sankaku yari was therefore best suited for penetrating armor, even armor made of metal, which a standard yari was not as suited to.[4] There are two types of sankaku yari: sei sankaku yari, yari blades with a triangular, equilateral cross section, and hira sankaku yari, yari with a triangular, isosceles-shaped cross section.

Ryō-shinogi yari, a blade with a diamond shaped cross section.

Fukuro yari (袋槍, "bag" or "socket spear") were mounted to a shaft by means of a metal socket instead of a tang. The socket and blade are forged from a single piece.

Kikuchi yari (菊池槍, "spear of Kikuchi") were one of the rarest types of yari, possessing only a single edge. This created a weapon that could be used for hacking and closely resembled a tantō. Kikuchi yari are the only yari which use a habaki.

Yajiri nari yari (鏃形槍, "spade-shaped spear") had a very broad, "spade-shaped" head. Yajiri nari yari often had a pair of holes centering the two ovoid halves.

Jumonji yari spearhead with metal collar; note the long tang, approx. equal to the blade-length

Jūmonji yari (十文字槍, "cross-shaped spear"), also called magari yari (曲槍, "curved spear"), looked something similar to a trident or partisan, and brandished a pair of curved blades around its central lance. It is occasionally referred to as 'maga yari' in modern weaponry texts.

Jogekama yari, a jūmonji yari with one side blade pointing down and one side blade pointing upwards.

Karigata yari, a jūmonji yari with the two side blades pointing down.

Gyaku yari, a jūmonji yari with the two side blades resembling a pair of buffalo horns.

Kamayari (鎌槍, "sickle spear") gets its name from a peasant weapon called kama (lit. "sickle" or "scythe").

Katakama yari spearhead owned by Kato Kiyomasa. Muromachi period, 16th century, Tokyo National Museum

Kata kamayari (片鎌槍, "single-sided sickle spear") had a weapon design sporting a blade that was two-pronged. Instead of being constructed like a military fork, a straight blade (as in su yari) was intersected just below its midsection by a perpendicular blade. This blade was slightly shorter than the primary, had curved tips making a parallelogram, and was set off center so that only 1/6 of its length extended on the other side. This formed a rough 'L' shape.

Tsuki nari yari (月形槍, "moon-shaped spear") barely looked like a spear at all. A polearm that had a crescent blade for a head, which could be used for slashing and hooking.

Kagi yari (鉤槍, "hook spear") was a key-shaped spear with a long blade with a side hook much like that found on a fauchard. This could be used to catch another weapon, or even dismount a rider on horseback.

Bishamon yari possessed some of the most ornate designs for any spear. Running parallel to the long central blade were two 'crescent moon' shaped blades facing outwards. They were attached in two locations by short cross bars, making the head look somewhat like a fleur-de-lis.

Hoko yari, an old form of yari possibly from the Nara period (710–794),[13] a guard's spear with 6 ft (1.8 m) pole and 8 in (200 mm) blade either leaf-shaped or waved (like keris); a sickle-shaped horn projected on one or both sides at the joint of blade.[14] The hoko yari had a hollow socket like the later period fukuro yari for the pole to fit into rather than a long tang.[15]

Sasaho yari, a broad yari described as being "leaf shaped" or "bamboo leaf shaped".[16]

Su yari ("simple spear") (alao known as sugu yari), a straight double edged blade.[17]

Omi no yari (omi yari), an extra long su yari blade.[17]

Makura-yari ("pillow spear")

Choku-yari ("straight spear")[18]

Variation Of Yari Shifts

A yari shaft can range in length from 1–6 metres (3 ft 3 in–19 ft 8 in), with some in excess of 6 metres.

Nagae yari ("long shafted spear"): 16.4 to 19.7 ft (5.0 to 6.0 m) long, a type of pike used by ashigaru.[19][20] It was especially used by Oda clan ashigaru beginning from the reign of Oda Nobunaga; samurai tradition of the time held that the soldiers of the rural province of Owari were among the weakest in Japan. Kantō was a chaotic place; Kansai was home to the Shogunate, and the Uesugi, Takeda, Imagawa, and Hojo clans, as well as pirate raiders from Shikoku. Additionally, Kyushu was home of one of the most warmongering clans in Japan, the Shimazu clan. Because of this, Nobunaga armed his underperforming ashigaru soldiers extra-long pikes in order for them to be more effective against armoured opponents and cavalry, and fighting in groups and formations.

Mochi yari ("hand spear"), a long spear used by ashigaru and samurai.[21]

Kuda yari (管槍, "tube spear"). The shaft goes through a hollow metal tube that allowed the spear to be twisted during thrusting. This style of sojutsu is typified in the school Owari Kan Ryū.

Makura yari ("pillow spear"). A yari with a short simple shaft that was kept by the bedside for home protection.[22]

Te yari ("hand spear"). A yari with a short shaft that was used by samurai and police to help capture criminals.[23]

www.ingramcontent.com/pod-product-compliance
Ingram Content Group UK Ltd.
Pitfield, Milton Keynes, MK11 3LW, UK
UKHW021935190726
13853UKWH00004B/1455